Tricks of the Rich

Tricks of the Rich

How to make, grow and save money

Paul A. Overy

Prentice Hall Business
is an imprint of

PEARSON

Harlow, England • London • New York • Boston • San Francisco • Toronto • Sydney • Singapore • Hong Kong
Tokyo • Seoul • Taipei • New Delhi • Cape Town • Madrid • Mexico City • Amsterdam • Munich • Paris • Milan

PEARSON EDUCATION LIMITED

Edinburgh Gate
Harlow CM20 2JE
Tel: +44 (0)1279 623623
Fax: +44 (0)1279 431059
Website: www.pearsoned.co.uk

First published in Great Britain in 2010

ISBN: 978-0-273-73635-6

British Library Cataloguing-in-Publication Data
A catologue record for this book is available from the British Library.

Library of Congress Cataloging-in-Publication Data
Overy, Paul A.
Tricks of the rich : how to make, grow and save money / Paul Overy.
p. cm.
ISBN 978-0-273-73635-6 (pbk.)
1. Finance, Personal. 2. Wealth. I. Title
HG179.0864 2010
332.024--dc22

2010029931

10 9 8 7 6 5 4 3 2 1
14 13 12 11 10

Illustrations by Ken Lee.
Typeset in 10/14 Plantin by 30
Printed by Great Britain by Henry Ling Ltd., at the Dorset Press, Dorchester, Dorset

Contents

Examples

Introduction: What the rich know and what you need to know

I'm writing this in May 2010 and in the last 24 months everyone's understanding of finance has had to change dramatically. But the process of knowing the right things and making the right financial decisions is the same whether the economy is booming or busting. Taking my home of Ireland as an example: we had close to 20 years of unprecedented economic growth (remember the Celtic Tiger?) and yet, it seems that few people actually added much to their personal wealth. They drove nicer cars and changed them more often; they traded up their homes; they took better holidays. They look better off, but they are not. In a recent speech in Dublin, I made the following comment: 'We have just had 20 years of economic growth that we may never enjoy again, and yet the vast majority of people I meet have come out of that period with only debt to show for it.' My remark was met with grumbles and the nodding of heads. This is the simple truth, a truth that has been experienced throughout the western economies. Does it apply to you?

What's my story about knowing the tricks of the rich?

I've worked in the financial services industry since leaving school in 1980, but you may be surprised to learn that I really only began relatively recently to understand money, and how it can be used to create what I call 'financial freedom'. I learned this fairly late in life, but financial freedom is what the rich know, and this is what you're going to learn about in this book. Some of that new-found understanding came from reading books but much more came from the lessons learned as my partners and I, through Financial Engineering Network Ltd (the financial advisory business I established in Dublin with two friends in 1996), helped our clients to achieve financial freedom for themselves.

For nearly as long as I can remember, I had an ambition to be *rich.* I can trace that ambition back to 13 February 1971, the day before decimalisation was introduced in Ireland. I was 9 years old and my grandmother owned a sweet shop close to the beach in Portmarnock, north of Dublin city. The next day all of the currency we had been using up to that time was to become obsolete. My grandmother had a pile of halfpennies on her kitchen windowsill and my younger brother, David, and I eyed these coins for quite some time, considering whether we might get away with taking one or two. Our courage grew and eventually we swiped one each and transported our ill-gotten gains to the competitor sweet shop close by. Our reward was two cigar chewing gums, which we chewed on the steps to the beach until our jaws ached, then we returned to the windowsill and repeated the exercise. This went on for most of the day, until the pile of halfpennies was gone and David and I could hardly speak for pains in our faces. That was the day when I learned that the more money I had, the more nice stuff I could buy. From then on, I stated an ambition to be *rich.*

Whenever I mentioned my new ambition, the adults around me would smile and tell me that as long as I worked hard, one day I would achieve my goal. And I believed them. Later, I was told that, to achieve my ambitions, I not only needed to work hard, but I also needed to work for myself. And I believed that too. After 12 years of working hard for other people, I eventually set up my own business and worked even harder. Three years later I had lost a large amount of money and was poorer than I had ever been. It seemed that the advice I had been given was flawed in some way. I had worked harder than most people I knew; I had set up my own business so that I would be the master of my own destiny, and 15 years after leaving formal education I was a pauper!

This is when I learned the point that I want you to understand – it's what the rich know and what you need to learn: the financial advice system that prevails in the western world is fundamentally flawed. Most people, no matter where in the western world they earn their income, end their working lives as relative paupers.

To take an example from Ireland: in the recent global recession Ireland Inc was hit particularly badly, with tax receipts falling to lows that no one had predicted or expected. Following the fall in tax income, the Irish government was left with a giant hole in its finances and had both to cut spending and raise taxes. One of the areas in which they sought to cut spending was the health service. During the two decades of growth and prosperity that preceded the recession, Irish citizens over the age of 70 had been granted free medical care and it was suggested that this would be removed. To ensure that this was implemented fairly it was decided that a means test would be introduced, so that only those who could afford to provide adequate care for themselves would lose the benefit. The results of the means testing surprised everyone: 95% of free medical care recipients would keep their benefits. Put another way this means that 95% of Irish citizens over the age of 70 need state handouts to keep themselves alive.

Is this what awaits the vast majority of us? Once we stop earning, we face relative – and, for many, real – poverty. This is true whether we work hard or simply do enough to get by, whether we earn a lot or a little, whether we work for ourselves or are employed by someone else, and whether or not we take the financial advice that is on offer.

So, how can it be that the vast majority of us end our working lives with a lifestyle that is frugal and unfulfilling? When there is so much wealth in the world and, frankly, so many opportunities to create long-term financial security for ourselves, how is it that so few of us take advantage of them?

What the rich know, what you need to know and how this book is going to help you

For me, the first step to creating my own financial freedom was the realisation that what I had been told about the route to financial success, both by the adults in my life when younger and by the so-called financial advisers as I entered the world of employment, was fundamentally wrong. As I met and dealt with more and more 'rich' people I came to understand that they deal with their money in a very different manner from most of us – after all, they are getting a very different result, so they must be doing things differently.

Throughout the book I share with the reader many of the lessons I have learned (some of which have cost me dearly), so that you can avoid the mistakes I have made as you attempt to reach your financial freedom.

This book is going to teach you what the rich know – the tricks of the rich. It'll give you the financial intelligence to begin to understand and then take control of your money. Your time will be needed, not only to read the book but to take the actions necessary to move forward on your journey towards financial freedom. It is the time that you are willing to give to your money, and managing it, that will make the difference in the long run.

In addition, I hope to impress upon you the fact that much of what you think you know about money is incorrect. If you are happy with the financial results in your life, then you may have no need to read this book or no need to alter the way you do things. However, if you are unhappy with the results and if, when you look into the future, all you see is a retirement of sacrifice and relative hardship, then recognise that only you can make the changes necessary to deliver a different result.

Who owns the money?

You may have heard the statments that '97% of the world's wealth is controlled by 3% of the world's population'. While this is a modern statistic, it struck me that it would have been just as true had it been written a year ago, 10 years ago, 100 years ago or even as far back as when the Pharaohs sat on their thrones in ancient Egypt. Throughout human history, the vast majority of the world's wealth has been owned and controlled by a tiny minority of people.

In ancient times, the way the wealthy maintained their grip on the wealth is well documented: they used violence and fear. While most of you reading this book are no longer exposed to the threats of this type of violence, we have to recognise the simple fact that, whatever methods the people with all the money are using to maintain their control, they are just as effective as those of the Pharaohs. Could there be a *great financial conspiracy* that keeps the riches firmly in the grasp of the elite few and ensures that we, the masses, spend our lives fighting over the financial crumbs from their tables?

The answer to this question has to be 'Yes'. To maintain the disproportionate distribution of wealth throughout millennia, those with all of the wealth must be acting in a manner to maintain the status quo. Surely it would be impossible for the inequitable distribution to have been maintained for so long without such effort?

Money, of course, is an extremely important part of our lives and, because it is so important, a massive and powerful industry has been built up around it. One of the 'Eureka' moments of my financial life came when I realised that the institutions (banks, insurance companies, fund management companies, etc.) that have been built up around this vital commodity are, in the first instance, there to make profit for themselves and their shareholders, not to make profit for their customers. I say this neither as a criticism nor in an attempt to discredit these institutions but to point out a simple fact. If you were a shareholder in any of these businesses, this is what you would expect of them – to deliver profit to you and not to concentrate on making their customers money. Sure, if clients become well-off by investing with, or borrowing from, the institution, you would have no objection to this but, as a shareholder, your first concern is profit for the institution and for yourself. These institutions have a vital role to play as you attempt to create your own financial freedom, but only when you learn the tricks of the rich.

This does not mean that we should not use the services of these institutions, but it does mean that we should avoid taking their advice! Since the primary objective of such institutions is their own profit, you can immediately see that they have a conflict of interest when attempting to give advice that makes you profit. Their financial products are designed with the institution's own margins to the fore, with client value for money necessarily in no better than second place. Unfortunately, for most of us, such institutions (and their agents, whether they work directly for the institution or are independent agents paid by the institution) have, to date, been the sole source of financial advice. Thus, it is no wonder that so few people ever reach financial freedom.

Consider this for a moment. While money is an extremely important part of modern life, we all go through an average of 12–20 years of formal education and are taught little about the subject.

While in more recent times a number of subjects dealing with economics, accountancy and other financial matters have been added to the curriculum, these concentrate on broad financial topics and teach students little about how to manage their money to create financial security. The introduction of Economic Wellbeing and Financial Capability to the National Curriculum for English and Welsh secondary schools recognises the need for greater financial awareness.

So we leave formal education and enter a financial world for which we are woefully ill-equipped. This lack of preparation is what drives us to seek advice, and the manner in which that advice is given ensures that the profit and wealth of the owners of the advisory businesses is put before our own.

When I gave the first draft of this book to friends and colleagues to read, most were very surprised by the comments on the subject of financial advice. As you read on, questions will be posed as to whether you have ever received genuine advice and some of my early readers thought I was being too tough on the financial institutions.

such institutions are fantastic product-providers; they are not fantastic advisers

So, to avoid any demonisation of these institutions, let me say it again loud and clear, such institutions are fantastic **product-providers** and, in my view, nobody can work effectively towards financial freedom without using their products. However, they are not fantastic **advisers** (no matter how much they purport to be) and you should not be taking advice from them. The reasons for my views will become very clear as you read on.

It is noticeable that the rich learn about money themselves and never depend upon large institutions for advice. They pay professionals to give them impartial advice, but there is no doubt as to who the professional is working for.

the rich learn about money themselves and never depend upon large institutions for advice

What the rich do, and what you'll need to do

In my experience, despite the importance we attach to money, we give very little time to the subject. We grab a couple of minutes here and there to concentrate on our own finances – but usually only when some form of problem has become apparent.

We all recognise that, to succeed in any walk of life – whether in sport, business, the arts, etc. – requires dedication, knowledge and/or talent and we all acknowledge that to hone these skills requires practice and diligence. Creating the very best financial future possible from your circumstances can only be achieved with the same dedication of time, the same knowledge accumulation, the same passion and ambition that you bring to so many other areas of your life. The simple fact is that, other than through blind luck (and, in my experience, there is as much bad luck out there as there is good), financial freedom cannot be achieved without effort and knowledge. This book will, hopefully, give you much of the knowledge – but only you can supply the effort. Good luck!

Paul A. Overy
May 2010

We have taken great care to ensure that the tax rates and examples given in this volume are in line with up-to-date legislation. However, tax law changes regularly so you need to check, in advance of taking any action, the tax rules and regulations that apply at the time.

Please note that throughout the book 'his' and 'him' have been used to apply to both genders for the sake of brevity and is not intended to exclude female readers.

Chapter 1

What is financial freedom? Why the rich have it and how you can have it too

Back in April 1996, together with two good friends, I started a business named Financial Engineering Network Ltd. Up to this point, all three of us had worked in the life insurance industry, mostly in front-end sales. In Ireland, this is the industry that delivers most of the investment and financial planning products, selling a range of investment vehicles, such as unit-linked funds, pension plans and life and disability insurance.

Each of us, over time, had become disillusioned with the industry, coming slowly to the conclusion that, although we carried business cards with fancy titles like *Financial Consultant* or *Financial Adviser*, we were not financial advisers at all, but merely product-sellers. In hindsight, I cannot understand how we ever believed ourselves to be financial advisers, since being paid a commission to sell a product is blatantly product-selling. This was a difficult realisation for us, as not only had we been proponents of such financial advice, but we had also been users of the products and services of our employers. However, our own financial results were undeniable: none of us had built any sustainable wealth and thus we had to abandon the methods of the past and come up with something new.

Deciding where you want to be

The first task we set ourselves was to define the financial goal, for ourselves and for our clients. Most people (including ourselves in 1996) do not have a defined financial target and, without that starting point, it was all but impossible to put a plan in place.

Consider your route to financial freedom as a journey you are about to take in your car: if you do not have a destination in mind, how are you ever going to get there?

As we came together to form our new business, we decided that we wanted to be true financial advisers to our clients and that, to deliver on this goal, we would have to build a service that the public would want to buy. We locked ourselves away in a darkened room and attempted to answer the following question:

> When it comes to financial planning, what are people trying to achieve?

The first thing we realised was that the ambition for most people was not great wealth: they simply wanted to have enough to live their chosen lifestyle. Great wealth comes at a price and, for many, the price to be paid is far too high. Take a look at the world's super-rich and then ask yourself whether they are happy. In truth, most people I have met with great wealth have sacrificed too much for their money. They may have failed marriages; they may have poor relationships with their children; they may have turned to drugs, promiscuous sex and, more lately, way-out religions to seek the happiness they so desperately crave. Is this the life most people want, or would they be happier if they simply had enough to keep themselves and their loved ones happy, healthy and safe?

Financial freedom

Over many days we debated and considered, made decisions and then reversed them, until we eventually came up with the concept of **financial freedom**. Yes, we all agreed, that was it; financial planning's ultimate goal was the achievement of financial freedom. We defined financial freedom as follows:

financial planning's ultimate goal is the achievement of financial freedom

> Reaching a stage where your investment assets can replace your lifestyle income without the necessity to continue working.

Whether you have defined your long-term financial goals in exactly these terms is unimportant. When I say these words to people, no one has ever replied, 'That is a rubbish idea'. Most do what you probably did when you read it: nod their head and give a wry smile. I interpret these two reactions this way: the nodding of the head recognises the desirability of the goal (who does not want to be financially free, after all?), but the wry smile questions whether such a wonderful outcome is possible. I can assure you that this goal is achievable for all, no matter what your income or age, although there is effort required from you to achieve it.

I am reminded of a story a work colleague told me recently. While in his golf club, he overheard two players having a conversation before going out for their round. One was complimenting the other on what he recognised as vast improvement in his game. The second man thanked his colleague for the compliment and told him it was all down to the lessons he had taken and the practice he was putting in. The first golfer thought about this for a moment and said, 'I am not good enough to practice.'

The attitude displayed in this one simple statement tells me why this man's golf will never improve: he is not prepared to put in the work that is necessary for improvement and he does not believe he ever will improve. My experience is that, for the most part, we get what we believe we will get in life.

But you can succeed

If you have the same attitude to money and the creation of your own financial freedom, then you might as well close this book right now and give it to someone else. That way, it may not prove a total waste of money.

Anyone, no matter what their income level, can apply the ideas and structures outlined in this book and learn the tricks of the rich. Nevertheless, like the improving golfer in the story, you will have to be prepared to change the way you have done things and to practise new techniques.

One of the differences I have noticed between truly successful people and the rest is that they have a burning desire to achieve their ambitions. Of course, anyone can recognise the attractiveness of financial freedom, but it is what you are prepared to do to achieve it that will dictate whether you are successful or not. This 'burning desire' is the key.

So what will you do with your financial freedom? You need to give some time to this question, plan what you will do the day you no longer have to work. The ambitions my clients in Financial Engineering shared with me were as varied as the people on the journey: working for a charity; spending more time with the family; collecting stamps; motor racing. Whatever it is you decide, be sure you truly want it, that you have a passion for it and that, within reason, you are willing to do anything to achieve it. If you are married, talk to your spouse to see if he or she shares the same dreams – certainly, there is little point in you taking a journey that your family do not wish to take. Then you will be ready to take your journey.

Starting the journey to being financially free

As with many life-changing events, the journey towards financial freedom starts with a look backwards to see where you have come from.

In Table 1 opposite I have set out a ready-reckoner. This will give you an idea of how much you will have to accumulate to achieve your financial freedom target. The assumptions used are outlined at the top of the table. These are: inflation will run at 3% per annum (this means that your assets will have to rise by this amount each year, simply to keep the same 'real' value); that the return you will get on your accumulated funds is 4.5% per year (which assumes a low-risk investment to house your funds when the financial freedom figure is achieved). Furthermore, the figure has been calculated assuming that you will live for 10 years beyond current normal life expectancy.

Later, I will outline for you how to calculate your lifestyle income (the income you spend on yourself: food, clothing, light and heat, transport, holidays, etc.). If your plans for the future include activities that are not part of your current lifestyle, estimate the costs and add these to your current lifestyle figure.

Once you've decided how much you'll need, or want, each month, simply find this figure in the left-hand column of Table 1, decide what age you would like to be when you achieve financial freedom (see the appropriate Target age column) and look down for the figure that tells you how much you need to accumulate to have financial freedom. For example, if your income requirement is £2,000 per month and you want to be financially free from age 55, then you need £507,178, whereas if your income requirement is £5,000 per month and you want financial freedom at 60 then you need £1,049,635.

Table 1 Calculating your financial freedom figure

Assumptions:		
Inflation		3%
Fixed interest growth rate		4.50%
Average life expectancy		
	Male	75
	Female	80

Desired monthly income (£)	Target age				
	45	50	55	60	65
1,000	331,990	294,206	253,589	209,927	162,992
1,500	497,985	441,309	380,384	314,891	244,488
2,000	663,980	588,412	507,178	419,854	325,984
2,500	829,975	735,515	633,972	524,817	407,480
3,000	995,970	882,618	760,767	629,781	488,976
3,500	1,161,965	1,029,721	887,561	734,744	570,472
4,000	1,327,960	1,176,824	1,014,356	839,708	651,968
4,500	1,493,955	1,323,927	1,141,151	944,672	733,464
5,000	1,659,950	1,471,030	1,267,945	1,049,635	814,960
5,500	1,825,946	1,618,134	1,394,740	1,154,599	896,456
6,000	1,991,941	1,765,237	1,521,535	1,259,563	977,952
6,500	2,157,936	1,912,340	1,648,329	1,364,526	1,059,448
7,000	2,323,931	2,059,443	1,775,124	1,469,490	1,140,944
7,500	2,489,927	2,206,547	1,901,919	1,574,454	1,222,441
8,000	2,655,922	2,353,650	2,028,714	1,679,417	1,303,937
8,500	2,821,917	2,500,753	2,155,508	1,784,381	1,385,433
9,000	2,987,912	2,647,856	2,282,303	1,889,344	1,466,929
9,500	3,153,907	2,794,959	2,409,097	1,99,308	1,548,425
10,000	3,319,902	2,942,062	2,535,892	2,099,271	1,629,921

This gives you an idea, perhaps for the first time, of what income-producing assets you will require to fund your financial freedom. Once you have a financial target, and a burning desire to achieve that target, you have taken the first step to putting a real financial plan in place. If the figure you calculate is not here, that's fine – you can work it out, and all the other figures will be proportionate.

This is a key trick of the rich, that it's important for you to learn. Like the golfer in our story, who practises, the rich know that they need to work at managing their money, and they know how much they want to have.

Because so few of us are in any way familiar with the world of finances, you are probably going to need the services of a real financial adviser, so before looking at some of the actions you can take to save money immediately, the next chapter is dedicated to helping you choose the right adviser for you.

the rich know that they need to work at managing their money, and they know how much they want to have

Chapter 2

Be advised like the rich and be advised by the right adviser

As I've mentioned, the fact that most of us enter our working lives with little or no knowledge of money means we are dependent upon getting advice from others. Although I am a firm believer in being like the rich and learning as much about money as you possibly can (hence, I have produced this book on the subject), I am also a realist and I recognise that to implement some of the structures that are described here, you will require outside assistance. So one of the first processes you may have to go through is choosing an adviser.

Even if you know everything there is to know about the financial world, an adviser may prove useful. In my own advisory firm, when meeting a potential client for the first time, I sometimes say: 'It is a 24-hour-a-day job to earn the money you earn and to have a life. It is also a 24-hour-a-day job to manage your money to achieve financial freedom and to have a life. Even if you know all that I know, where will you find the time to do the second job?'

The typical answer is probably the one you are thinking of right now: 'I will not be able to'.

So, as I often said to potential clients who give me this answer: 'I am applying for the second job.'

How do you pick the right adviser? What tricks can the rich teach you about advisers?

Avoid 'free' advice

The first thing to do is to get a list of all fee-based advisers in your area.

But, I hear you ask: 'Why do I need to pay a fee? Isn't free advice available?'

Yes, there is much available that purports to be 'free advice', but it is *not* advice! If you are getting 'free' advice, then either you are getting that advice from a charitable institution or it is 'free' because someone else is paying the adviser. I am unaware of any institution in the financial planning world that operates in a charitable fashion and, therefore, if you are getting (or seek out in the future) 'free' advice, then it is probably because someone else is paying.

> if you are getting 'free' advice, then it is probably because someone else is paying

Do you know the saying, 'He who pays the piper calls the tune'? The rich know that this is just as applicable to financial advice as it is to anything else. You need to be paying your financial adviser, otherwise he/she may well be playing to someone else's tune.

For some reason, the selling of financial products and services, for most of us, is not considered selling at all – but, of course, it is! People paid a commission to sell us something, whether it is clothes, computer repairs or financial products, are salespeople; they are not advisers – no matter what their business card says. Just as a shopkeeper will not tell you that you can buy a better product at a lower price in a competitor's shop, neither will a bank salesperson tell you about a competitor bank's product, even if the competing product is better.

Those who offer 'free' advice are often paid a commission by the financial institutions that they represent. I call this kind of commission-remunerated advice *biased* and the rich know this too. No matter what your financial circumstances or requirements, salespeople will always try to sell you something – otherwise, they will not get paid. If you are attempting to create financial freedom, biased advice is to be avoided.

Avoid isolated advice

From the list of fee-based financial advisers that you've put together, you need to identify one who can deal with all aspects of your finances.

I do not mean that this person must do everything for you, but they must be able to consider your entire financial situation when giving advice. Otherwise, you may suffer the inefficiencies that isolated advice can cause. Your new adviser needs to prove to you that he/she has the knowledge to take any and all of the following into account as his advice is formulated.

- tax (both corporate and personal, covering income and capital taxes)
- investments (both on-shore and off-shore)

- risk evaluation
- mortgages and other loans (personal and corporate)
- retirement schemes (both private and 'off-the-shelf' versions)
- pensions
- life and health (all types) insurance
- legal issues
- succession planning and wills
- property (residential, commercial and retail).

It's important to remember that your new adviser needs to be able to discuss each of these areas with some degree of expertise, simply because these subjects have the potential either to increase or decrease your wealth. I know it may be difficult to find one person with such breadth of knowledge and experience, but it should be easier to find a firm that will satisfy your requirements. So, in looking for an adviser, you should probably be looking for a firm of advisers, and thus you could discount any one-man-bands on the list.

> isolated advice can be detrimental to the creation of long-term financial security

I'm going to emphasise that you need this full range of expertise because I have so often witnessed how isolated advice can be detrimental to the creation of long-term financial security. I am sure that many of you will have heard the saying that my grandmother quoted nearly every day of her life: 'Look after the pennies and the pounds will look after themselves.' The problems caused by isolated advice generally affect the 'pennies' and, in my experience, many people ignore them because of the relatively small amounts involved. But these small amounts accumulate – and can cost you big-time!

Let's view it another way. Your attempt to create financial freedom is like attempting to fill a wooden barrel with water. The barrel has a few small leaks, but you are able to get water in much more quickly than it leaks out, and so you succeed in filling the barrel to the brim. Congratulations! You've achieved your goal. But as we know, reaching the goal is only one part of the task; once you reach it, you want to maintain it. If you do not fix the leaks, then your water, however slowly, will drain away. And so with your finances – if you do not fix these leaks, no matter how small they are, eventually your assets will drain away. Also, I find that the very act of fixing the 'small stuff' in our financial world is extremely educational and means that such inefficiencies are unlikely ever to creep into your world again.

Financial inefficiencies and what to do about them

Let me give you an example of the type of financial inefficiencies that isolationist advice can lead to.

I'm hoping that none of you would be foolish enough to walk into a bank and borrow money at a rate of 9% per annum (that's the fee they charge you to borrow money), and then cross the foyer and put the borrowed money on deposit at 3% per annum (that's the fee a bank would pay you to borrow *your* money). However, if the clients that I advise are typical of the population in general, at least half the people reading this book do exactly that.

The problem is that most people separate these two transactions by time and institution – you make the two decisions at different times and with different advisers (or salespeople perhaps?) – so that you borrow money to buy a car on one date and, several months later, when a bonus comes your way, you tuck it away in a deposit account for a rainy day. The effect is the same: you are paying a higher interest rate on your borrowings than you are receiving on your savings, and you are borrowing your own money and paying for the privilege!

I understand why so many people make this mistake: not every financial decision is part of an integrated plan and time dulls the memory. We make financial decisions on the run, grabbing moments here and there to think about, and take action with, our own money and rarely, if ever, does our last (or second last, or third last …) financial decision impact on the one we are making right now.

However, if you have a good financial adviser in your corner, who knows your financial circumstances inside out and who has the experience and expertise to help in all areas of your financial life, then you will not make these mistakes and financial inefficiencies will not erode your pennies.

Other inefficiencies that could be keeping you from truly starting to generate financial freedom include:

- failing to take advantage of all tax concessions
- earning your income in an inefficient manner
- misunderstanding risk and reward
- taking financial advice from those paid commission to sell you 'stuff'
- investing only in what you know, without making any attempt to expand your own knowledge
- accepting loan offers that are structured to the lender's best advantage, rather than your own

- making offshore investments without fully investigating (and thus understanding) all the tax implications
- avoiding the world's stock markets because you fear them
- over-accumulating assets in your own name and, by so doing, substantially increasing the taxes to be paid by your heirs
- borrowing for consumables
- not borrowing for investments
- failing to make a will and thus leaving the distribution of your assets to the state.

The list of potential inefficiencies could go on and on, but I will not labour the point any more. There is one more item I will add, however:

- failing to make, and to revisit, a plan.

Make a plan

When choosing your financial adviser, you now know that he/she must be fee-based and must demonstrate an ability to add value in all areas of your financial life. This probably leaves you with quite a short list of prospective advisers. I suggest it is time to go meet those remaining.

your financial adviser must be fee-based and must demonstrate an ability to add value in all areas of your financial life

The first thing that I would insist upon is that any adviser worthy of consideration must mention a **plan** and explain how they would work with you to achieve that plan.

The main reason for writing this book is to demonstrate to the reader that creating financial freedom is as much about the 'hows' (*how* you act with, and around, your money), as it is about the 'whats' (*what* type of investments you use). The first 'how' is *how* to choose the right adviser. Working to a plan allows both you and the adviser to judge progress easily, simply by asking yourself regularly: 'How are we doing with regards to our goals?'

Your first meeting with each of your short-listed advisers should cost you little or nothing. As an adviser, I always offered the first consultation for free. After all, I did not know whether I could help someone until I met with them and heard a little about them. If I did not yet know whether I could help, the potential client did not know either and, in such an engagement, I could not justify a fee.

At this first meeting, expect the adviser to give you a broad history of his business and details of the expertise of the firm's staff. Expect him to ask some probing questions (without yet seeking in-depth and private information), to get a broad picture of your current financial circumstances. Then you should be told what the adviser believes he can do for you and how much you can expect to pay for the first phase. You should not make a decision on the spot, and if the adviser is pushing for an immediate decision, personally I would walk away and cross them off my list.

Remember the following rich trick, and

- Ask for all details discussed at your initial meeting to be confirmed in writing and on the headed paper of the adviser.
- Ask for a copy of the firm's fee schedule and their terms and conditions of business.
- Ask for client testimonials from people who have already dealt with the adviser, including, if possible, one you can get verbally by contacting the person directly.
- Tell the adviser when they can expect you to make your decision on whether to engage their services. In my opinion, the adviser should be aware you are shopping around.

Once you have visited all of the advisers on your short list and have gathered the relevant information, you are in a position to make your final decision. Probably, there will be one adviser who stands head and shoulders above the rest, so, if you go through the process described, it's likely that your adviser will have picked himself.

Chapter 3

A few simple money-saving ideas to get you started

I know nothing specific about your particular financial circumstances but I am sure that the money you currently spend on financial services and products is not being spent to your best advantage.

> avoid borrowing your own money and paying for the privilege

The first money-saving rich trick I want to give is one we have mentioned already: avoid borrowing your own money and paying for the privilege.

For those of you still shaking your heads and thinking: 'Don't be ridiculous, I would never do that!', assume that you have taken out a 9% loan (for, say, £20,000, over five years) to buy your car. In isolation, this is a very good deal. Generally, such debt is on an unsecured basis, linked to a depreciating asset, so 9% in such an environment is not too high a price. Now, two years later, another adviser suggests that you save towards the cost of your children's future education (and so you are paying £300 per month at present). The advice is to do so via a long-term deposit-type vehicle with a large financial institution. Again, viewing this in isolation, a 3% guaranteed return with no risk to your capital, from a financially secure source, is also a good deal. In isolation, both financial decisions are good ones; both advisers have done their jobs effectively and within their respective compliance regimes.

In this scenario, you would be better off if you stopped saving money and, please excuse the pun, accelerated your car loan repayments. You would save thousands in interest payments, and could return to saving money when the loan has been paid off. The example below, taken from a real-life situation, illustrates how you can ensure that your money is working for you, and not for the institution.

Example 1

Borrowing and saving

A car loan was taken out two years ago for a total sum of £20,000, which is repayable over five years and charged at an interest rate of 9%. The monthly cost of servicing this loan is £428.49.

The total cost of this loan, over the five years, is £25,709.40 (£428.49 × 60 months) and, after two years , the borrower still owes capital of £13,015 which, with interest, will cost £15,425 to repay.

Two years after the car loan was negotiated, the same person decides to save £300 per month in a deposit account and receives 3% per annum interest. In the next three years (the same period as remains outstanding on the car loan), he will earn £514.38 in interest on his savings.

Instead of saving the £300, what will happen if he 'invests' that money into the car loan, paying £728.49 each month? Paying more off the loan each month will shorten the repayment term – in this case, reducing it from the remaining 36 months to only 19 months.

The cost comparisons of this action are:

Overall **cost** if loan left untouched:

£428.49 × 36 = £15,425.64

Overall **cost** if loan accelerated:

£728.49 × 19 = £13,841.31

By 'investing' the additional £300 each month in the car loan, the borrower saves interest payments of £1,584.33 (the amount *not* paid out on the car loan), while losing only £514.38 in interest foregone on the deposit. The net gain of £1,069.95 is equivalent to an annual return of 20.3% on the £300 per month 'investment'.

And the benefits are even greater over the longer term as, in this example, the borrower was also trying to make provision for his children's education. By investing the £300 each month in the deposit account and maintaining the car loan repayments on their normal schedule, the deposit balance would be £42,027.23 after 10 years. But, by paying off the car loan early and returning to saving money when this is done and then paying £728.49 per month (car loan payment + saving of £300), he will accumulate a total of £68,182.69 in the deposit account in the 10 years, some 62% *more* than if the current structure is allowed to continue.

This example shows that, if you pay attention to everything going on in your financial world, you can massively increase the value for money you're getting in both the short term and the long term.

Another rich trick it also illustrates is that, once you get used to paying out a specific monthly amount, you should continue to pay out the same amount, even after the original debt has been cleared, since this will add considerably to your financial freedom. Most people, once the loan above had been repaid in full, would simply spend the £428.49 per month that's now available on more 'stuff' – since lifestyle spending always rises to meet available income, if you allow it to do so.

You can see that a simple review and restructure of existing investment activities can make you wealthier. You need to review everything you have done in the past – and I mean everything. Placing money on deposit and borrowing money to buy consumer items are two areas where most people make expensive mistakes. Let's take a look at each in detail.

Deposits

I cannot remember where I read this, but it is said that, in the UK, you are more likely to get divorced than to change your bank. Even in Ireland, where divorce rates are lower, the same principle applies. You can be absolutely sure that your bank knows this and will use it to its own advantage.

it is said that, in the UK, you are more likely to get divorced than to change your bank

In my experience, when anyone has a lump sum to deposit, it typically ends up in their existing bank and they take whatever rate the bank says is available. There are two problems with this approach:

- It is rare that an ordinary clearing bank will offer the very best rate on the market. Such institutions are generally extremely large, with heavy fixed overheads, such as staff and a branch network, and demand a higher margin than a smaller institution. This means that they offer less in returns to their customers than others.
- The investor does not haggle, but simply takes the first price that is offered. I do not know why most people believe they cannot haggle when it comes to financial products. I know people who will haggle over the price of everything but money. My advice is to haggle your socks off. The rich haggle and it will pay dividends.

my advice is to haggle your socks off. The rich haggle and it will pay dividends

At the time of writing, interest rates are low, yet smaller deposit-takers are offering rates of 1% and, in some cases, even 2%, more than their high-street competitors. A 1% or 2% increase in annual returns may seem small, but it may be an effective 100% or greater increase in returns. And even greater gains are to be made if you are willing to commit your money for a fixed term. But let's look at what an increased return can achieve for you in the longer term. In Figure 1, I'm going to

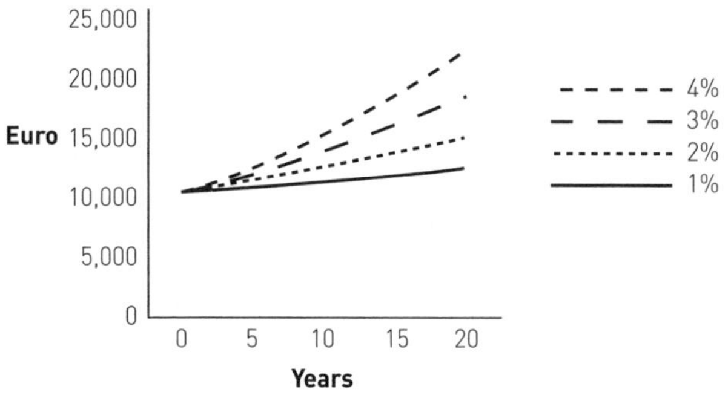

Figure 1 The future value of £10,000

* All figures rounded up or down to the nearest £5.

look at the difference in future capital, over different timeframes, for an investor with £10,000 to place on deposit.

As you can see, reasonable increases can be enjoyed if you are willing to haggle over price. For example, over five years, getting 2% per annum instead of 1% per annum increases an investor's wealth by £530 – or, expressed another way, by almost 104% (the return at 2% is £1,040, 104% of the return at 1%, which is £510).

I have not taken tax into account; suffice it to say that the after-tax returns will be just as improved as the pre-tax figures illustrated here.

Consumer debt and credit cards

The rise in popularity of the credit card and/or store card, along with other forms of consumer goods finance has had the most profound influence on the distribution of wealth in the western world. The ease with which such credit is made available has enhanced its popularity as a method of raising finance, while the rates charged have actually served to make the banks and major stores richer and you, the consumer, poorer. This type of debt should be repaid in advance of any other.

Interest rates can be 17%+ per annum. At the time of writing, my own credit card charges me 17.1% per annum in interest on outstanding balances – although, as you might suspect, I don't carry long-term outstanding balances. To put these rates in perspective - it means that an item purchased for £1,000, that you pay for over two years, actually costs you nearly 19% more. To repay £1,000 over two years, at 17% per annum interest, will cost you £49.44 per month or £1,186.56 over the term (£49.44 × 24 months). So you can see that paying an interest rate of 17% actually increases the real cost by considerably more than 17%. At £1,000, your purchase may well be value for money; at 19% more, it is likely that you are simply paying too much.

Of course, many of you reading this do not need me to point out the obvious. We all know that credit cards and other such cards are expensive. Why is it then that you still have outstanding amounts on your card (or, in some cases, cards)? I mentioned at the start of this book that you would have to change some of your beliefs and opinions about money to achieve financial freedom. But simply changing beliefs is not enough; you have to change the way you act too. Instead of choosing the easy option and, when your next credit card statement arrives, simply paying the minimum, pay it all! Organise an overdraft or loan, if you have to. After all, these can be half the price, if not less, of credit cards. Then, once it's all paid off, get rid of the credit card. Of course, they are handy and more secure than carrying cash but they stand between you and your financial goals. Replace them with a charge or debit card, which is just as handy and secure, but which is automatically repaid from your bank account each month (this means that you never run up long-standing balances on which you pay continuing interest).

changing beliefs is not enough, you have to change the way you act too

We have all been allowed by the lenders to think that we can have the trappings of wealth before we are wealthy. Easy access to debt on credit cards, car finance, personal loans for holidays, allows us to enjoy things immediately without stopping to count the cost.

The true cost: think about the costs, benefits and risks

To make any financial decision to your best advantage you need to be in possession of three vital pieces of information:

- the costs
- the benefits and
- the risks.

So, if you are really serious about being like the rich and achieving your goal of financial freedom, then you need to identify each of these when making any financial decision, whether that's spending, saving or investing money. In truth, our lack of financial education, combined with the complexity of the financial system, means that we very often make financial decisions thinking we have the information, when we really do not.

Let me give you an example of what I mean. I know I am labouring this point, but it is one of the most important I make in this book because if you get your consumer debt under control, your route to financial freedom will be far easier. I want to look at how you fund the purchase of a car.

if you get your consumer debt under control, your route to financial freedom will be far easier

Ever since it first appeared, the motorcar has been a sought-after status symbol. Why do you think the rich have such nice ones? Not only are the manufacture, sales and maintenance of motorcars multi-billion-pound businesses, but they have spawned other multi-billion-pound businesses such as car accessories, car magazines and model cars. We seem to be infatuated with the motorcar and the purveyors of credit know this all too well.

When my father was in his early career, back in the 1950s, the acid test as to whether he could afford a car or not was: 'Do I have the cash?' Somewhere between then and now, the car manufacturers and the banks have convinced us that the question is: 'Can I afford the monthly repayments?' This new attitude has served the manufacturers and banks very well indeed. The problem is that the true cost of buying a car does not form part of the decision-making process, principally because most of us have no way of calculating that cost. The following example outlines the true cost.

Example 2

The true cost of buying a car

Assume that the car has a retail price of £30,000 and that this amount is borrowed over five years at an interest rate of 8%.

The monthly repayments on the car loan will be £626.14.

So the overall cost of the £30,000 car is (£626.14 × 60) = £37,568.40.

But, that's not the true cost of the car. You pay this money out of taxed income, which means that you will have had to earn more in order to pay the tax too. The personal income tax rates you pay on your income will dictate the true cost. For illustration purposes I have assumed two simple rates of 20% and 40%; your cost may be higher or lower than these, depending upon your top tax rate.

So, the actual cost of your car, from your gross (that's your salary before tax) income, is £782 per month for five years if you pay a 20% tax rate and £1,044 per month if you pay the higher rate. Putting it another way, for a person earning £40,000 per annum, agreeing to this loan means pre-spending between 23.5% and 31% of each of the next five years' income before it is ever earned.

And that's still not the true cost of the car, as you could have invested the £782 or £1,044 each month over the five years without any tax liability whatsoever (see Chapter 4 for details), instead of buying the car. And, assuming that such an investment achieved a 5% per annum return, it would have accumulated in five years to between £53,400 and £71,300.

The decision to buy the car has meant that you are £53,000/£71,000 less well-off at the end of the five-year period than if you had invested the money instead.

Of course, if you really need to buy a car, then you have no choice but to incur this expense, unless you have the cash. However, a huge percentage of new cars are bought by people who already have a car and who are trading it in to buy a newer, flashier model – these people have a choice. Either way, my point is that the purchase of a car (or other major item) should be made in the knowledge of its true cost. So, the next time someone asks what your car cost you, use these figures to calculate the true cost. If your car was bought (with 8% finance) for £15,000, then its true cost was more like £26,700/£35,650; if it cost £60,000, then its true cost is £106,800/£142,600. This is the amount of money, based on the assumptions outlined earlier, that you would have accumulated had you chosen to invest towards financial freedom instead of purchasing the car. All other figures will adjust proportionately.

Earlier, I wrote about the need for you to change some of your financial habits and there is no doubt that the habit of funding the purchase of luxury consumer items with short- to medium-term debt is one of the worst you can have. Resolve to stop it today. Where possible, accelerate the repayments on any existing consumer debt and save yourself thousands in interest payments. In the future, do not buy these items until you can afford them – that is, until you can buy them the old-fashioned way, by paying cash. And the next time you are tempted, for there is nothing more sure than that you will be tempted, remind yourself of the real cost of these items when bought with consumer debt – hopefully, that will keep you focused.

ask questions that ensure you get the numbers before you make a decision

Most people, when they see the car loan numbers for the first time, are shocked. They simply did not realise the true costs of the transaction, and so made a decision without one of the three vitally important pieces of information. I am not for a moment suggesting that you immediately become a whiz at financial calculations, but you can ask questions that ensure you get the numbers before you make a decision. When you know the **costs**, you can compare them to the benefits and make a fully informed decision.

Chapter 4

The golden rules of the rich

The first three chapters have concentrated on some relatively simple changes you can make to ensure that, when you make a financial decision, you give yourself the very best opportunity to enjoy the very best possible outcome. We have looked at changing the way you go about taking 'advice', and ensuring you make your borrowing decisions knowing all you need to know about the true cost of the finance. Applying what you have learned will not be easy, as it requires you not only to change the way you think about money but, more importantly, to change your habits – habits that are not financially productive but comfortable all the same. Einstein's definition of madness was: '... doing the same thing over and over again and expecting a different result'. The way you have thought about and managed your money in the past has not made you financially free, and if you continue to manage it that way you are likely to end up as a relatively impoverished senior citizen. If you want a different result in the future, you are going to have to do things differently from now on.

If you stopped reading now, and simply applied what you have learned so far to your own circumstances, you would be a good deal better off when you retire than you would otherwise have been. But to really make a difference to your present and future financial existence, you need to master the Golden Rules.

These 'rules' are used by the rich to create wealth, because they understand that the end result of any financial decision has as much to do with *how* you take an action as it does with *what* action you might take.

Golden Rule No. 1: Borrow to create financial freedom

one of the real tricks of the rich is that they often make their money with other people's money

One of the real tricks of the rich is that they often make their money with other people's money. They use debt simply as a tool with which to build their financial future. As you read on, you will see that the introduction of debt has the potential to seriously increase the returns on your investments, even if debt is not needed.

Good debt and bad debt

I want to emphasise that the debt referred to here is not consumer debt. In my experience, people's view of debt can be polarised: some people will borrow as much as a bank will let them have (no matter what is being purchased with the money) and some, quite simply, will not borrow for anything.

Like most things in life, the issue is not black or white. Debt is neither bad nor good in itself: it is the use you make of the money that dictates whether you add to, or subtract from, your personal asset value. 'Bad debt', as far as this book is concerned, is debt that offers no potential for you to get wealthier – we saw some examples in Chapter 3. 'Good debt' is debt that offers potential for you to get wealthier; it is raised for investment purposes, where the investment itself offers the potential for returns greater than the real cost of the finance.

debt is neither bad nor good in itself

I started my working life in 1980 and, since then, the average net asset value of most people in the western world has been rising steadily. For the most part, this is not because we are saving more or investing more prudently – not deliberately, at least – it has been the product of our love affair with property. For example, 79% of the Irish adult population own their own home[1] and in the UK 70% of people own their own home. Of course, people have bought these homes with someone else's money – with the lender's money. As the underlying value of the property has risen at a pace greater than the cost we pay to the bank, we have been getting wealthier. In most cases, this growth in our wealth has been achieved without any real effort or worry on our part. The house was bought 'because we liked it' and the lender's money was used because 'that is the norm'.

Let's look at the wealth that a typical Irish homeowner would have accumulated over those 20 years. I'm using an example from Ireland, but similar figures would also apply to the UK. In 1985, the average family home in Ireland cost €46,542.[2] Typically, this would have been purchased with a 90% home mortgage, with the bank providing €41,888 and the borrower putting up the extra €4,654. Assuming an average home loan interest rate over the term of 5%, the cost of this 'investment' in cash outlay terms was:

- Deposit: €4,654
- Average monthly loan repayment: €280.10

(Note: I use the Euro currency here but the mathematics is the same whether you use British pounds, American dollars – or any other currency, for that matter.)

The value of this average house had risen to €264,472 by 2005, which means that, had this property been purchased for cash at the outset, the return to the purchaser would have been 9.08% per annum.

However, the fact that the homeowner used the bank's money has increased his real gains. Since he did not buy for cash but borrowed 90% of the purchase price, there was a cash outlay of

1 *Source*: Central Statistics Office, *Census 2002*.

2 *Source*: Irish Department of the Environment, Heritage & Local Government, 2005.

€4,654 on Day 1 and then 240 payments of €280.10 per month. Although this gives a total cost of €71,878, the timing of the payments means that the investor has achieved a real return of 10.44% per annum. The 'good debt' used by our investor has increased the annual return by 1.36% or, in other words, by 15% in total. By using the lender's money instead of his own, our clever homeowner has achieved an increased return, not by buying a different property or by investing more money, but by simply paying attention to *how* the property was bought.

The more recent and well-documented fall in property prices would, of course, affect the return the purchaser has enjoyed, but that in and of itself is of little importance to the point being made. If we assume that the value of the 'average' property has fallen say by 30% from the 'highs' quoted earlier, it is now worth €185,130 – still *more* than was paid originally – and so the mathematics will deliver similar benefits. The point being made here is that **debt** itself, due to the fact that it means the purchaser does not have to come up with cash up-front, is making the investment *more* profitable for the investor.

This example illustrates that debt ('good debt') has a major role to play in your future attempts to create wealth. What surprises me, as I talk to people who have benefited by borrowing for the purchase of their home, is that when I recommend they do the same thing with investment property, they somehow perceive a far greater risk. To be truthful, the financial risk is higher with your home than for a rental property. Not only do rental properties offer similar capital appreciation potential to your home, but they produce income too! When you borrow money for your home, you must repay the loan, in its entirety, from your own income. When you borrow money for an investment property, you are able to repay at least some of it with rent from your tenant (i.e. with someone else's income).

good debt has a major role to play in your future attempts to create wealth

Returning to our previous example for a moment, let's assume that the property was bought as an investment, using the same 90% loan/10% cash deposit, and that the investor had averaged a rental income of €125 per month, net of tax. The cost of the property then would be €41,878 (the €4,654 initial outlay and 240 out-of-pocket payments of €155.10 per month – the actual monthly payment less the net rental income the investor received) and the investor's real annual return would have grown to 13.64% – a 50% increase!

So, as you can see, by changing *how* you make an investment, and introducing debt as a tool to accelerate the rewards, you can massively increase your return. Of course, there are *risks* here, additional risks than when simply buying for cash. Indeed, you could say that it is the risk of borrowing that, in our historical example, is delivering the additional gains. The property is the same, the interest rate assumptions are the same, *only* the risk being taken has changed. At times, investment debt is easily arranged; at others it is all but impossible to raise (the credit crunch being a very good example), but loan availability does not alter the mathematics. No matter whether the economic environment is 'booming' or 'busting', the maths is still in the investor's favour.

by introducing debt as a tool to accelerate the rewards, you can massively increase your return

I am not for a moment suggesting that the economic environment has no affect whatsoever, but careful planning in advance of making an investment decision will ensure that you do benefit. I personally have a number of investment properties, all purchased with investment loans, which recently have seen serious drops in value. However, I can afford the monthly repayments, the tenants are still paying their rents and so the value of my properties today is of little importance; my sole concern is their value as and when I am targeting to reach financial freedom. You see, in advance of accepting the loan offer, I did the calculations. Over any extended period of time, my expectation is that my properties will rise in value (inflation will make sure of that, I suspect), but I am also painfully aware that, over relatively short periods of time, the valuations can fall too. I wanted to be sure that I could sustain my loans in such an event, so I did not simply accept the loan because I could afford the monthly repayments, I stress tested the mathematics in advance.

The people who are losing money right now are those who did no such testing, who bought property on the false assumption that it always goes up in value or that interest rates do not fluctuate. They are the ones who find themselves unable to pay the loans, unable to sell the properties and thus losing huge amounts. They lose money when they are forced out of the investment; anyone who can ride out the economic turmoil and await the inevitable recovery does not lose at all. So, when you raise finance, do not simply make your decisions based on the current economic environment, for although I am not a clairvoyant, I can confidently predict that it will change.

do not simply make your decisions based on the current economic environment

Releasing equity to create new investment assets

Now, armed with the knowledge that investing other people's money can work for your own gain, you need to look for opportunities in your current circumstances. Many of you reading this book will already own your own home and will have sizeable equity built up in that property. The 'wealth' that this equity represents is useless, unless you decide to put it to work on your behalf. Many of us make the mistake of thinking that our homes (for the majority of homeowners, their home is by far their most valuable possession) can contribute to our financial well-being. Unfortunately, this is not true unless:

- You sell your home at some stage in the future and downsize
- You use the equity you have built up to re-mortgage and invest in income-producing assets.

Your home is, of course, an asset, but it is not one that can contribute to your financial freedom. A 'financial freedom asset' is one that produces income, while a 'financial freedom liability' is one that consumes income. I know which one best describes my home and I imagine it is the same for you – our homes consume our income!

During a recent conversation with my dad, this subject arose as we were discussing his assets. 'Your house is not really your asset,' I told him, 'It is mine.' At first a little perturbed by my statement, his concern faded as I told him that his house does not contribute to his income – indeed, it consumes his income. 'However,' I explained, 'It will contribute to my income when I inherit it.' He conceded that I was correct – that, while his home was valuable, it produced nothing tangible for him or my Mum (other than a place to live, of course).

If, as an existing homeowner, you do not use your house to create financial freedom assets, then you will end up like my dad – and, I imagine, so many other dads – asset-rich and cash-poor. Remember, financial freedom and thinking like the rich is about having enough income-producing assets to replace your lifestyle without the necessity to work. Not only does your home not produce income, it consumes income. So, if you want to be financially free, you have to do something about it.

not only does your home not produce income, it consumes income

Selling your home in the future and downsizing to a less expensive property can allow you to create income from this asset. But I believe that the luxuries you have worked so hard for in the past should be maintained and so my preference is the equity release system. Let us look at an example.

Let us assume you have a home valued at £500,000, on which there is an outstanding mortgage of £100,000. So, your equity stands at £400,000 and a 10% rise in property values produces a 12.5% rise in your wealth. In other words, when the value of your home rises by 10% (from £500,000 to £550,000), you realise £50,000 (12.5% increase) in additional wealth from a £400,000 investment.

Many lenders are happy to grant investment loans on a 70% loan-to-value basis and are willing to take your home as security for such finance. This means you should be able to raise a total debt of £350,000 on your £500,000 asset, giving you an additional £250,000 (once you have paid off the existing mortgage) to invest.

This £250,000 can now be used as a 30% deposit on a new property, which should allow you to invest around £830,000. At the end of this process, you will have total property assets of £1,330,000 (a £500,000 home and an investment property worth £830,000).

Of course, overall, your property wealth has not altered. You own £1,330,000 in property and owe £930,000 (£350,000 borrowed against your home and £580,000 borrowed for the investment property), thus you still have £400,000 in net assets. Now, however, if the value of your properties (note the plural) rises by 10%, your wealth increases by £130,000 – a 32.5% increase on your investment of £400,000.

'Ah yes,' I hear you say, 'But what about the rent? Will my tenant pay? Will the rent be enough to repay the loan or will I have to add money from my own pocket? What about property values in the future – will they continue to rise? What about tax – will it simply erase all of my profit?'

All these are valid questions and all need to be answered satisfactorily before you take any action. Of course, some of these questions arise out of fear and it's normal to be scared of the unknown. The questions about the future rise (or fall) in property values and about a reliable tenant are more related to risk than fear. And you do need to consider risk against potential profit.

Don't let fear paralyse you when it comes to financial matters. You have already seen the potential that this idea has to generate real wealth into the future and do not forget that risk is an essential part of becoming financially free. The rich know this, and you need to learn it. I have said it before, but I'll repeat it: if you are not prepared to take some risk, stop reading now. You are simply wasting your time and there are far more enjoyable and entertaining books awaiting you in the fiction section of your local bookstore or library.

> risk is an essential part of becoming financially free. The rich know this, and you need to learn it

If you can overcome this fear, if you can force yourself to raise good debt in the pursuit of real investment assets, then the next money-saving idea involves how you repay that debt.

The proper repayment structure creates even more wealth

Most people are uncomfortable with large debt (and yet the same people think nothing of having sizeable outstanding credit card balances on which they are paying interest of 17%+ per annum) and rush to repay their investment loans. This may not be the best use of your money!

In Ireland, there are full tax deductions on the interest payments when the loan is for investment property (some other forms of investment activity also attract such tax relief) and you need to ascertain whether the same type of tax concession is available where you earn your income. Assuming it is, what this means is that, insofar as the rent you receive on your investment property (or properties) is used to repay interest on your loan, that rental income is tax-free! This is a huge tax benefit and sizeably reduces the real cost of repaying interest of this nature. Despite this fact, lenders typically do not provide loans that allow borrowers to take full advantage of this concession.

Capital and interest repayment loans

Most investment loans are issued on a 'capital and interest' basis, which means that the bulk of your monthly payment is used to pay the interest on the loan; the balance is used to pay down the capital borrowed. As you repay the loan, less and less of your annual payments are interest – as the outstanding loan reduces, the interest also falls, leaving more in each monthly payment to pay down capital, which in turn reduces the interest and so on. But this means that, as the years roll by, more and more of your rental income is exposed to tax and, in real terms, the debt becomes more expensive to service.

Example 3 below shows the capital and interest repayment method, illustrating the annual costs of repaying a £250,000 loan over a 15-year period on a rental property. The property costs £280,000, inclusive of all costs, so the borrower must put up £30,000 in cash. I have assumed a rental yield (that's the money you'll get from your tenants) of 5% per annum (£14,000), which stays constant throughout the loan term (in reality, you would expect some increases in rent over the years) and an interest rate of 4% per annum. I have also assumed a personal tax rate of 50%, which may be higher or lower for you. The question then is: what is the after-tax cost of this property?

Example 3

Capital and interest repayment loan

Loan

Loan amount:	£250,000
Term:	15 years
Interest rate:	4%
Income tax:	50%
Loan type:	Capital and interest (annuity)
Annual payment to lender:	£22,485

Income	
Annual rental income:	£14,000
Average annual tax:	(£4,090)
Average annual after-tax rental income:	£ 9,910
Overall cost to investor	
Annual repayment (capital + interest) to lender:	£22,485
Average annual after-tax rental income:	(£ 9,910)
Average annual after-tax cost:	£12,575

Tax rates vary dependent upon the extent of your income and the manner in which that income is earned. As with all examples used in this book, you will need to check the benefits you can enjoy based on your personal tax liabilities.

Because the percentage of your monthly repayment that is interest is falling each year, the real cost of a capital and interest repayment loan such as this is rising each year. This is due to the fact that you have fewer and fewer tax deductions and so pay more and more tax.

I am not for a moment trying to put you off investing with capital and interest debt. As long as the property rises in value over the 15 years, you will make substantial profit, even if you use this repayment structure. If we assume a 5% annual increase in the value of the property,[3] then if it is worth £280,000 today, it should be worth £582,100 in 15 years' time. Selling for this price would give you an annual return of 10.17% per annum over the term. While this is a good return, there may be other methods of repayment that allow you to reduce your tax liabilities substantially and, in so doing, to reduce your out-of-pocket costs and thus increase your real profit.

There are two mortgage types worth considering:

- interest-only loans
- retirement-backed loans.

[3] Although we saw earlier that Irish residential property had risen by 9.08% per annum from 1985 to 2005, it always pays to be conservative with your future estimates.

Interest-only loans

Some lenders, depending upon the property being purchased and the overall financial proposition presented by you (the borrower), will lend to property investors on an interest-only basis.

As its name suggests, this type of loan allows you to repay just interest; you do not repay the capital at all. The idea is that, when the property is eventually sold on, you repay the capital.

The advantage of this type of loan is that, in our example at least, it may be possible to purchase an investment property that, on an ongoing basis, costs you nothing in out-of-pocket terms. Example 4, which uses the same underlying assumptions as Example 3, illustrates how this loan works.

Example 4

Interest-only loan

Loan	
Loan amount	£250,000
Term:	15 years
Interest rate:	4%
Income tax:	50%
Loan type:	Interest only
Annual payment to lender:	£10,000
Income	
Annual rental income:	£14,000
Average annual tax:	(£2,000)
Average annual after-tax rental income:	£12,000
Overall cost to investor	
Annual interest payment to lender:	£10,000
Average annual after-tax rental income:	£12,000
Average annual after-tax cost:	(£2,000)

Tax rates vary dependent upon the extent of your income and the manner in which other income is earned. As with all examples used in this book, you will need to check the benefits you can enjoy based on your personal tax liabilities.

As the figures in this example illustrate, and assuming you live in a jurisdiction that allows tax concessions of this nature, it is possible to service the loan and to generate extra income of around £2,000 a year (the difference between rent received and payments to the lender).

Using the same capital growth assumption as used earlier, selling the property in 15 years' time for £582,100 would mean an average return of 22.3% per annum – 12.13% per annum more than by repaying the loan on the conventional capital and interest basis. In this example, the clever investor increases the return to 220% of what it would have been by changing *how* the money is borrowed. The interest-only structure has one other advantage – it allows you to buy more property, since the cost of servicing the loan(s) is lower. However, interest-only has one main disadvantage too: you have to sell the property to repay the loan (to get the yield above, you have to unlock your cash and the only way to do this is sell). Becoming financially free is about keeping the wealth you create and, therefore, this method is not advisable if you wish to keep the property long-term, hence the reason for showing you one more option.

Retirement-backed loan

The interest-only method is more lucrative than the conventional capital and interest repayment method, due to the fact that it makes use of the tax law and avoids capital repayments altogether. The savings are made because the borrower can use his rental income to pay all the interest and gets an additional £166.67 per month into the bargain. Savings are also made as the borrower no longer has to pay tax on any capital repayments. Consider it this way: if you pay 50% income tax and have to repay a £250,000 loan out of after-tax income, the cost to you will be £500,000 in pre-tax income. You have to earn the half-million, pay tax on it and then give back the money to the lender. The interest-only method avoids that problem by planning to repay the debt after the property is sold. The retirement-backed method delivers similar rewards, but this time uses a retirement plan to accumulate the capital repayments so that you may keep the property rather than have to sell it to unlock your gains.

You have already seen how greater tax efficiency can hugely improve the returns you receive, thus increasing your wealth and speeding up your journey to financial freedom.

greater tax efficiency can hugely improve the returns you receive

The ordinary capital and interest method both exposes more of your rental income to tax and requires repayment of capital out of after-tax income. In contrast, the retirement-backed structure allows you to accumulate the capital repayment with tax-free money too.

In essence, this repayment structure uses the interest-only facility from the lender, alongside which you have a retirement plan. Most retirement structures around the world offer substantial tax advantages to those who use them; if you do not know your own entitlements may I suggest that you ask your financial adviser as soon as possible. Inside the retirement plan, you accumulate a tax-free lump sum of £250,000 (continuing our previous example) net, which matures in 15 years and is then used to repay the loan. Example 5 illustrates the costs.

Example 5

Retirement-backed loan

Loan

Loan amount:	£250,000
Term:	15 years
Interest rate:	4%
Income tax:	50%
Loan type:	Retirement-backed
Annual payment to lender:	£10,000

Income

Annual rental income:	£14,000
Average annual tax:	(£2,000)
Average annual after-tax rental income:	£12,000

Retirement contribution

Annual pre-tax payment:	£15,660*
Annual tax savings:	£7,360*
Annual after-tax cost:	£8,300*

Overall cost to investor

Annual payment to lender:	£10,000
Annual after-tax cost of retirement contribution:	£8,300
Average annual after-tax rental income:	(£12,000)
Average annual after-tax cost:	£6,300

*I have used the Irish retirement allowances here; you will need to get an idea of the tax allowances in your jurisdiction so as to accurately re-create this example for yourself.

Tax rates vary dependent upon the extent of your income and the manner in which that income is earned. As with all examples used in this book, you will need to check the benefits you can enjoy based on your personal tax liabilities.

When compared to the capital and interest structure, this method is estimated to save you almost £80,000 over the 15 years. This improves your yield (once again assuming the property is valued at £582,100 at the end of the loan term) from 10.17% per annum to 14.3% per annum.

Thus, simply by paying attention to the *way* you repay your loans, you can vastly increase the profits you make. Obviously, this repayment structure is more costly over the 15 years than the interest-only alternative. However, the big advantage of this method is that, because the retirement plan pays off the loan, the property will continue to create income and capital gains long after the loan is repaid, whereas with the interest-only method, the property has to be sold to get your profit.

What I hope I have shown you in **Golden Rule No. 1** is one of the key tricks of the rich. They know that debt is a tool, a device that can bolt a 'turbo charger' onto your investment returns. I have also shown you that it is the type of loan, and the tax treatment of interest and capital repayments, that will dictate the true costs of your finance. Lenders are not usually quick to offer these types of loan, as frankly they do not deliver more profit to them. You know now that the banks and other lenders have no interest in your profitability, so it should not surprise you that lenders typically structure loans to reduce their own risk and raise their profits. You need to question them at every turn, ask for the loans that best suit you and your financial ambitions and stop thinking that all loans are the same. You have seen that it is simply not true. Lenders are just purveyors of money, nothing more or less, although many people seem to think of them as demi-gods. In truth, if one bank will lend you money, most banks will lend you money; there is no such thing as loyalty or favours in the banking business (other than the loyalty we show our banks). By insisting that you speak with a number of lenders, you will create competition for your

stop thinking that all loans are the same

business and this will drive down the costs and/or improve the terms and conditions you are offered.

At times, let me warn you, lenders may try to argue that the retirement-backed structure increases your risk and will attempt to convince you to stick with the ordinary capital and interest structure. They will point out that, for the retirement plan to actually repay your loan, it needs to create a certain investment return. While it is true that the plan does need to earn a specific return (in Example 5 above, the return was assumed to be 6% per annum), it is *not* true that this increases your risk.

In order to judge accurately the risk being taken, we need to ask how the retirement plan would have to perform for you to pay the same price as the capital and interest structure. In fact, in Example 5, the retirement plan could produce a return as low as 0.49% per annum (less than half of one per cent – about the same as you get from a bank deposit account!), and the overall cost would be the same. If the retirement plan delivers more than 0.49% per annum, you get wealthier.

Remember: when a lender talks of risk, they generally are not referring to your risk but to their own.

Golden Rule No. 2: Invest your money before you pay tax

If I asked you what you think your greatest financial liability is, you might say one of the following:

My home(s)	My hobby(ies)	________
My wife	My car(s)	________
My husband	My holiday(s)	________
My children	My pension	________
My golf club	My credit card(s)	________
My clothes	School fees	________

Is your answer here? If not, I have left spaces for you to fill in your own greatest liability. Do that now before reading on.

> tax is the greatest liability in your life, in my life and, indeed, in nearly everyone's life

Whatever you answered, unless you answered 'tax', it's incorrect. Tax is the greatest liability in your life, in my life and, indeed, in nearly everyone's life. The rich have recognised this, yet the rest of us have failed to see it.

Think about it for a moment. Every time you earn money you pay tax – and every time you spend money you pay tax. In the UK, income tax is charged at a top rate of 50%, in addition to which a National Insurance contribution is payable. What this means is that, at the top rate, we only get to keep less than half of what we earn. Then, when we spend this money, up to a further 17.5% tax is charged as VAT (due to be increased to 20% from January 2011). In the UK, as throughout the western world, at every turn, you are faced with a tax liability. Tax is the greatest liability in your life – and, therefore, it is the greatest obstacle to you achieving financial freedom. The rich know this and you have to learn it too!

What the rich have realised is that becoming financially free has little to do with how much you *earn* and everything to do with how much you *keep*! If you can make investments before you pay tax, then you will be keeping much more, even before you make a single penny on the investment. If you can achieve this, then you will have more money invested, for a longer time, and your wealth will grow considerably faster.

Pensions before tax? And why not?

It is relatively easy to invest at least some of your income before paying tax, via your pension. The tax allowances to which you are entitled are dependent on your income and you will need to check with your new financial adviser the tax benefits you can enjoy.

However, despite what is an extremely attractive tax break, most people do not use their full allowances in this area. Why are such substantial tax benefits being summarily dismissed by most people? Are you one of them? There are many reasons, which range from complete lack of knowledge on the part of the investing public to the inappropriate manner in which such products are sold. However, the most important explanations are these:

- As various pieces of retirement legislation have been passed into law, they have been hijacked by the financial institutions, which created 'pension plans'. You may have noticed that I have, until now, avoided the use of the word 'pension'. This is quite deliberate. A pension is an insurance policy, a vehicle laden with charges (some hidden, others more obvious) and delivered to the public by commission-remunerated salespeople. I believe that the general public has long been dissatisfied with the returns being delivered by the insurance companies and this has led, unfortunately, to throwing out the baby with the bath water. By refusing to pay the often exorbitant charges levied by insurers, you also close the door to the huge tax concessions. While the rich certainly do not purchase off-the-shelf pensions, they do use the tax concessions that retirement legislation provides.

- Many of us, whether experienced investors or not, are most comfortable when we can make our investment choices ourselves. Off-the-shelf pensions available offer little flexibility, with investment options typically limited to a range of 'own funds' offered by the insurer. Funds labelled 'Managed' or 'Equity' or 'Gilt' offer little in the way of choice and, to be truthful, most people I meet have no real idea of what they actually invest in. This lack of flexibility, coupled with the investor's lack of knowledge, has stopped many people from enjoying the tax concessions available.

If you are one of the many people who have never invested in a pension, or have dabbled but not used your entire allowances, then do not concern yourself too much. I happen to agree with your decision; the lack of transparency in such products (where charges are concerned), along with the 'one size fits all' attitude to investment that these plans take, makes them poor value for money. However, I do think that you should be taking advantage of the tax breaks and, like the rich, it is most likely that you can do so without having to buy a standard pension.

> legitimate retirement allowances are certainly the easiest tax break you will ever access

Legitimate retirement allowances are certainly the easiest tax break you will ever access and there is no question as to their effectiveness, or their authenticity. But retirement allowances are dictated directly by legislation and, as long as you do not invest beyond your personal allowance, you are *guaranteed* the tax break. Depending on which type of retirement fund you use, the allowance you will receive will depend on three things: your employment status, your age, and, on occasion, your gender (as women tend to live longer than men, their retirement allowances may be higher).

If you are self-employed or in non-pensionable employment, then the private pension fund accessible to you is sometimes known as a **self-directed personal pension (SDPP)**. The maximum allowance to which you will be entitled, i.e. the amount of pre-tax income you can invest, is dictated by legislation and by the use you have made of the allowances in the past. Tax relief is limited to contributions up to the higher of the following:

- 100% of your UK taxable earnings
- £3,600.

So, taking the lower figure as an example, you should be able to pay at least £3,600 per annum from personal income into a retirement plan.

Of course, such an investment does not cost £3,600 out of your take-home pay as you save considerable tax. By way of an example, let us look at how much it will cost out-of-pocket.

Gross annual contribution	£3,600
Tax savings @ 50%	£1,800
Net annual cost	£1,800

You can immediately see the second Golden Rule at work here: for a cost of £1,800 this investor has an investment fund of £3,600, which can now be placed in a range of investment assets including property, stocks and shares, deposit funds, land, etc.

If you are a proprietary director or a senior executive working for someone else, then the private pension fund available to you is known as a **self-administered pension fund (SAPF)**. The allowances available to an individual who falls into this category can be substantially greater than the SDPP (and it is here that the allowances for women can be higher than for men), a reason for many self-employed people to switch to limited company trading.

No matter which private retirement fund is available, such vehicles will not levy a multitude of charges on you. Instead, you pay a fee to establish the vehicle and an annual fee to administer and monitor the scheme. The annual fee should also cover auditing and compliance services for the year. Do not – and this is one of the attitude changes I referred to in earlier chapters – let a fee scare you off. Remember that, for every £1,000 you pay in a fee, a contribution of £2,000 to the scheme will save you £1,000 tax (assuming the 50% rate; other tax rates will increase or decrease this figure) in the next year. After the break-even point, every additional penny you save in tax is taking you that bit closer to your financial freedom goal.

There is one more benefit to using your retirement allowances in the manner I have suggested. Inside the retirement fund, your investments will be exempt from income tax (a retirement fund pays no income tax on its investments, whether income comes from dividends on shares, rental income on properties or deposit interest from financial institutions) and capital gains tax. Yes, you read that correctly – a retirement fund is exempt from income tax on any income your investments create and, if you make a capital gain, this too will be tax-free.

a retirement fund is exempt from income tax on any income your investments create

The rich use all available tax concessions; they keep more of their money for themselves and thus they can save more towards the future. The private retirement fund not only allows you to keep more of your regular income, but it also allows you to keep more of your investment income and investment gains too. Some tax will be payable later on and, while proper planning can reduce future tax liabilities too, in Table 2 opposite I have assumed the maximum amount of tax would be levied at the end.

Table 2 illustrates the power that tax-free investment has to make you wealthier. It is based on an annual income of £10,000, which is then invested. In the left-hand column, I assume that you pay tax on this income at 50% and invest the balance, while in the right-hand column, I assume you pay the full £10,000 directly into a private retirement fund. Obviously, if you invest in your own name you will pay tax on your annual profits, whereas the retirement fund pays no tax, so I have included tax within the personally-held investment. Tax will be levied once income is taken from the retirement fund, however, what we are interested in is the amount of cash that is being accumulated within the retirement fund when compared to the normal investment route. Note that you may receive 25% of your withdrawal tax-free, so tax is levied on 75% of the fund only.

Finally, I have assumed a 20-year investment term and a 6% per annum gross yield (yield before tax) in both situations.

Table 2 Personal investment *vs* private retirement fund

Personal investment		Private retirement fund
£		£
10,000	Earned income	10,000
5,000	Income tax	Nil
5,000	Annual amount invested	10,000
*150,530	Value of investment in 20 years, assuming 6% gross annual growth	389,930

Note: All figures rounded up or down to nearest £5.
* Here I have assumed half the annual growth would be achieved through capital appreciation (taxed at 18%) and half would be as income (taxed at 50%). The figures calculated assume the income tax liability is paid annually and has been calculated by reducing the annual yield by the tax payable.

So you can see that making investments the way the rich do can have a huge effect on your future wealth. Remember, both the left-hand and right-hand columns represent the same money, earned in the same way, invested in the same assets, producing the same annual rate of return. Simply by copying how the rich invest you have accumulated for yourself 159%+ more money!

Remember, once you reach financial freedom, you will not need a pension in the same way as others need a pension – it will simply be one of your assets that provides the complete financial security that financial freedom brings.

Act now!

Now that you know the Golden Rules, resolve today to do something with your new-found knowledge. You must take action – immediate action, in my view – for the longer you delay, the less likely you are to do something positive.

One thing the rich know is that they must always act sooner rather than later. This is another change you have to make if you truly wish to achieve financial freedom and live like the rich. Earlier, I suggested that you would have to change the way you think about money; you will have to change the way you act about money too. The simple truth is that most of us do not act at all; rather we react to financial issues and usually only when they have started to cause us some problem. Now it is time for positive action and, while I have no doubt that some readers will have the ability to act for themselves, most of you should seek out a truly impartial financial adviser. Remember the lessons of an earlier chapter, look for someone who will charge you a fee and who will listen to your wishes. 'Free advice' is an oxymoron (it cannot exist); if it is free then it is not advice, it is product-selling!

most of us do not act at all; rather we react to financial issues

Armed with the relatively basic knowledge that these first four chapters have given you, you now know more about money than most of the financial advisers I have ever met. Stick to your own agenda and find an adviser who will charge you a fee. (Remember to get references, preferably from existing clients – just because someone charges a fee does not mean they are good at the job.) That way, you know he works for you and has your best interests at heart. The rich will *only* deal with advisers that avoid the conflicts of interest caused by advisers' need to sell something to make money, and so should you.

Chapter 5

Borrow to create wealth, but borrow wisely!

Despite the fact that it was coined over 400 years ago, I am surprised by how many people live their financial lives by the saying, 'Neither a borrower nor a lender be'.

Shakespeare wrote *Hamlet* in 1592. In this play, Polonius offers the above advice to his son, Laertes, before the latter embarks on a long journey. Not only was it well-meaning but, back then it was also excellent advice as, failing to repay your debts could result in a swift introduction to the working end of a sword.

My own dad first quoted this mantra at me and he did so with the same love and care that Shakespeare's character was showing for his son. If it has been quoted to you as well, then whoever introduced you to this advice was also well-meaning; however, unlike in 1592, today debt is usually no longer a matter of life and death. You have seen in the previous chapter that borrowing is simply a tool, and the type of borrowing you negotiate has the potential to massively increase the profits you can create from a particular investment. Attempting to create financial freedom without borrowing is like setting off to run a marathon with your shoe-laces tied together. While it is possible to complete the race, it would be impossible to do so in any reasonable time and the most likely outcome is that you would grind to a halt somewhere along the course and give up.

attempting to create financial freedom without borrowing is like setting off to run a marathon with your shoe-laces tied together

When most of us hear 'Never a borrower or a lender be' what we really hear is 'Don't borrow money', but, of course, it also says 'Don't lend money'. If you need proof that the message is outdated and relatively useless in the 21st century, take a look at the value of the financial institutions that lend money. Throughout the world, most of the companies that are involved in lending money are the most valuable public companies. And even when these monolithic institutions fall foul of their own overexuberance, it is you and I, as taxpayers, that have to bail them out. Doesn't this emphasise the point that lending money can be worthwhile?

To return for a moment to the concerned father's advice in *Hamlet* – for 1592, he was correct and offered his advice to keep the son he loved safe. However, today, if your goal is to accumulate some wealth and financial security, this advice could actually undermine your ability to achieve it.

One of the real tricks that the rich use is that, once they create a little wealth, they borrow against it to create some more. You have heard the phrase: 'Money makes money'? In reality, the extended version of this is: 'Having some money allows you to borrow some more and investing the borrowings creates more money' – it just does not roll off the tongue as easily as the shortened version.

But isn't debt a bad thing?

Debt can be defined as either 'good debt' or 'bad debt' and, to avoid any confusion, in this chapter I am referring to the 'good' type. Good debt is where the debt is raised to make an investment that has the potential to make you wealthier; bad debt is generally debt raised to purchase a consumable, where there is no possibility of you getting wealthier. Where good debt is concerned, the following trick of the rich is absolutely true:

good debt is raised to make an investment; bad debt is generally raised to purchase a consumable

> As long as the return on the investment you make with borrowed money is greater than the cost of the debt, you are making money for free!

The rich know that it is the cost of debt that dictates the profit or loss they enjoy when borrowing to invest. This is true for them and it is true for you too. You simply need to master the art of identifying the costs of borrowing and negotiate with the lender so that these are reduced to their absolute minimum.

Working out the cost of debt

The way you repay investment debt makes a huge contribution to its true costs. The lower the effective cost of any such debt, the more likely you are to enjoy an investment return in excess of that cost. So, first of all, you must know the repayment structure that will deliver the most **profit** to you and you need to negotiate hard with your lenders to ensure you get that repayment structure.

Working out the likelihood of a particular investment outperforming the cost of your debt is how you go about judging the risk being taken.

How risky is risk?

Risk is like anything in life that causes you to feel fear. The fear itself generally comes from a lack of familiarity and understanding. As children, we fear the dark, we fear certain animals, we fear heights and large bodies of water but, as we become familiar with these things and understand them more, our fear lessens and, for most of us, all but disappears.

Fear can be a paralysing emotion. Making financial decisions with your emotions (the other active emotion being greed) is not the way to create financial security. What the rich know and what you must realise now is that, just as your childhood fears disappeared as your knowledge of the world and your own personal skills grew, so too your fear of debt risk will disappear when you understand it better and when your knowledge grows to allow you to judge, unemotionally, investment risk for yourself.

your fear of debt risk will disappear when you understand it better

The rich teach their children about debt, showing them how to identify the true risks of investing with borrowed money and giving them the knowledge and experience that the rest of us are so badly lacking. In this way they can take on borrowings while being fairly sure that all risks have been identified in advance, and this gives them the very best chance of a profitable outcome. If you too can identify all risks in advance, you can use this trick of the rich to your advantage.

Buying property as a way of borrowing wisely

As most of us buy property with borrowed money, we're going to look at the risks (and fears) that you may encounter when buying an investment property (with borrowings).

Risk 1 – Interest rates may rise

Obviously, when borrowing on a variable interest rate (one that changes as market interest rates rise and fall), there is the potential for the cost of the loan to rise.

The rich have the same problem as the rest of us, in that they too are subject to interest rate fluctuations, but they know how to look into the future and see where interest rates are heading. You can also do this by asking your lender to tell you their fixed interest rates over the next two, three, or even five years. If these are higher than the current variable rates, then you can be fairly sure that your lender believes that interest rates will rise in the future. If such rates are lower, then the opposite can be deduced.

Rather than simply failing to act because of your (uninformed) fear, why not ask the question and see whether your perception of rising interest rates is shared by your financial institution (and they are probably in a much better position to judge where interest rates are going than you are).

Even if rates are expected to rise, this does not automatically mean you should avoid borrowing. Instead, do your calculations on the property, asking your lender for the costs assuming the highest interest rate you have been quoted, and see whether, even in that worst-case scenario, you can still create profit. Doing this – and yet still borrowing on a variable rate – means that, even if rates rise to their predicted maximum, you have convinced yourself, before the investment is made, that you can handle the costs. Alternatively, you could choose to arrange your finance on a fixed-rate basis, which will mean that, for the duration of the fixed period at least, no matter what happens to interest rates, your costs will stay constant.

The credit crunch that gripped the world in 2008 meant that finance is more difficult to get. Also, the fact that many people who borrowed in the recent past are losing their properties through repossessions may affect how you perceive this type of risk. However, the reason those people are losing their assets is they failed to crunch the numbers *before* they borrowed. Borrowings were arranged based on 'I can afford the costs right now' and little or no thought was given to the future. Only those who lose their assets will lose in the longer term; anyone who can maintain the asset and await the inevitable recovery (and the economies of the world *will* recover, what cannot be yet predicted is *when* that will happen) will make money.

Risk 2 – The property may devalue

Again, it is perfectly possible that a property's value could decrease. We've seen this in the recent credit crunch. However, remember that true wealth creation happens *over the long term.* I find it impossible to contemplate an environment where property bought today would be less valuable in, say, 10, 15 or 20 years' time. Such an environment would require a catastrophic economic event or a series of such events. While that is possible, it is improbable in my opinion and, to be frank, in the event of such catastrophe, I imagine the last thing on my mind will be the value of my investment property!

> true wealth creation happens *over the long term*

The recent property devaluations around the world show that short-term circumstances can devalue property, but again it is *only* those who fail to *keep* the properties they bought that will lose in the long term. All property owners who can afford to await the recovery will eventually make money. I assure you that the rich will not be called out of their property investments because of bad planning and if you do your calculations correctly when making the investment, neither will you.

When buying a property as part of your attempt to create long-term financial security, the short-term capital gain or loss is irrelevant and the rich know this to be true. Much more important is judging the letting potential. This will help you decide how much of your own money you will be required to part with on an ongoing basis. The success of using a rental property as an investment will be dictated by how you choose the property to buy. The following tricks are used by the rich:

- In order to gauge what area will produce the most demand from potential tenants, they place a number of 'dummy' advertisements in the newspapers, offering for rent the type of properties they are considering purchasing in a number of different residential areas. They give a phone number with a voice-mail (so they do not have to deal personally with the enquiries) and, after a while, they count the number of enquiries in each location. This costs only a few pounds and immediately tells them where the letting demand is highest.
- They do the calculations based on a 10-month letting period each year and at the lowest rent that they have been told such a property will demand. In this way, they are making their decisions based on, within reason, a worst-case scenario and any post-purchase 'surprises' on finance should be positive.
- They visit an independent letting agent in the location being considered. Independent letting agents are not involved in property sales and make all of their income by letting other people's property. This means that they are less inclined to talk up a particular property (which could happen if the letting agent is part of the same organisation that is offering the property for sale). Letting agents only want properties on their books that they can let and, therefore, are a good source of advice for the investor, since they are unlikely to suggest the purchase of a property that they could not let and could not make money from.

Risk 3 – The tenants may default on their rent

This is potentially a problem for any landlord but one that can be managed by using a letting agent to handle your property. The agents will reduce this risk, as they will demand references from any potential tenant. While this will add a layer of cost to the transaction (I pay my letting agent 12.5% of the rental income I receive), it will massively reduce the 'hassle factor' of being a landlord, as well as reducing the risks.

No amount of preparation for any investment you care to consider will altogether eliminate the risks of fraud, but the more rigorous the checks you put your tenants through, the more you will weed out potential bad tenants.

While the use of a letting agent adds costs, the rich value their time very highly indeed and realise that if they did not pay an agent, then they themselves would have to do the work. I imagine that you are not looking for another job and so, by adding the costs of a letting agent into your calculations, you are considering all costs before making that investment.

By applying this trick of the rich, whether the market is booming or busting, you will only purchase a property that clearly demonstrates the potential to make you money. The more preparation and research you do in advance, as the rich do, the lower the risk and the greater the opportunity for you to make real profit.

Risk 4 – The maintenance/refurbishment costs might ruin my investment

From time to time, you will incur unexpected costs (leaking pipes, painting and decorating, etc), but you can reduce the risk by being diligent as you buy the property and by being prudent when you do your financial calculations.

Hire a qualified surveyor to give the house a once-over before you buy and that will tell you a lot. It will cost some money but the fee is likely to be less than one-quarter of one percent of the purchase price. For ongoing maintenance, set aside around 10% per annum of the annual rent to cover these costs and make sure you can still afford it, based on this assumption. Finally, recognise that such costs are legitimate expenses for any landlord and can be paid out of your rental income before tax is paid. For example, based on a top tax take of 50%, the real cost to you is only half of the actual costs – in other words, these costs will only be around half of what you expect them to be.

Remember too, the tricks you learned in Chapter 3, in that you are likely to have a loan repayment structure that suits you (and not just the lender). This is estimated to reduce the real cost of your loan (when compared to those who simply accept the bank's 'advice') by between 10% and 30%, possibly more. Integrating the new trick of good debt into your decision-making process will allow you to be more enthusiastic about a particular project than the investor who has to pay considerably more for the property.

It may surprise you that, if you have the cash available for a particular investment, my suggestion is that you borrow the money! This suggestion is made based on the assumption that the investment to be made is 'allowable for tax purposes' and thus you will receive a tax deduction against your interest payments. In an earlier chapter I demonstrated how many of us are borrowing our own money and paying a heavy price to the financial institutions. The rich are able, when borrowing is tax-deductible, to turn the tables on the lenders and to get a similar benefit for themselves. This is done by recognising that the true cost of tax-deductible debt is *lower* than the interest rate being charged. If, for example, you are paying interest of 5% on borrowings, but are able to repay this without paying tax (and rental income is tax-free as long as it is used to pay interest

the true cost of tax-deductible debt is *lower* than the interest rate being charged payments on the debt), then the true cost is substantially less. If you avoid 50% tax on the rent, the true cost of the interest is 2.5% *not* 5%. Placing cash on deposit may guarantee a net return of higher than this cost and so the rich can often be making money on the same money twice. This is a trick of the rich that you too may be able to use and should discuss with the advisers you choose to assist with this type of investment.

So, debt can be good?

In my experience, debt, like risk, is viewed by most people in a very black-and-white manner. Most assume that more debt means more cost and less income in their pocket, but this is simply not the case. At the very beginning of this book, I said that I would challenge your beliefs about money and thereby prompt you to think more like a rich person. If you have viewed all debt in a negative manner, if you have voiced the ambition to be debt-free, perhaps you need to revisit your attitudes and beliefs.

You can borrow for property and for the stock market

Borrowing has been available to purchase property for a long time, but it has proved more difficult for people to borrow for the other main investment you can make: in the stock market (equities).

I have long recognised the wealth that you can create by using other people's money and I have shown you the trick when it comes to buying property. However, equities tend to outperform property and I have always been keen that my clients could exponentially increase the returns from the stock markets, using the same method. The problem has been that lenders have not been very willing to lend to investors in the stock market. Even those who have provided loans for such investments have limited the amount of finance they provide. The highest loan-to-value ratio (LTV = the amount of borrowing expressed as a percentage of the overall security, e.g. a loan of £200,000 against a property worth £400,000 has a LTV of 50%) I have seen is 50% (whereas property investors typically receive 75% to 95% finance). But you can't necessarily fault the lenders for that. They are in the business of managing their own risk (not yours) and, other than property in the immediate vicinity of a disaster, it is hard to imagine a property (over which they take a lien to back the loan) dropping in value by 40% in a day. It is not quite so difficult to imagine shares dropping in value by such an amount in a day: there are very many historical examples of such devaluations.

The point is that it is not the absence of long-term potential in equities that has scared banks away from lending to investors so that they can invest in the stock market, rather it is the volatility of the value of the asset that frightens them. The vast majority of banks also are involved in equity fund management and are well aware of the potential of these assets to beat the market, but that awareness does not mean they want to risk their lending organisations. Remember that lenders, like bookmakers, are not involved in the risk business – they make very fine profits on a tried and tested, virtually risk-free, business model. Of course, there are times when a particular deal for a lender in isolation may be viewed as a risk but, overall, once they stick to their operational rules, the lender (or the bookmaker) is guaranteed to make money.

remember that lenders, like bookmakers, are not involved in the risk business

It was certainly frustrating, as a financial adviser, not to be able to link up the 'turbo-charger' (of making investments with other people's money) to the equity investment vehicle. We always knew that, if it were possible, the wealth creation outcome could be spectacular. That opportunity came into being with the arrival of tracker bonds, which offer capital guarantees and track the performance of equity markets: investors could borrow to invest and be sure that they cannot lose their capital.

Tracker bonds

The humble tracker bond has been around for many years and is a relatively simple product. A typical tracker bond, which always has a fixed term (three, five, six years, etc), is really two products in one:

- A certain amount of the money invested is placed on deposit and is guaranteed to grow back, over the product term, to the amount originally invested. The higher the interest rate available from the product provider, the lower the amount of money that has to be invested in the deposit element of the product. For example, imagine investing £100,000 into a tracker over six years. If the net of tax return available from the deposit provider was a guaranteed 3% per annum, then £83,748.43 of the £100,000 investment would be placed on deposit. If the deposit interest rate after tax was guaranteed to deliver 4% per annum, then only £79,031.45 of the £100,000 investment would be needed on deposit. In both examples, based on the assumed net interest rate, each amount would mature at a value of £100,000 after six years.
- Having underwritten the capital guarantee within the deposit account, the product manufacturer now has between £20,968.55 (£100,000 less £79,031.45) and £16,251.57 (£100,000 less £83,748.43) of the investor's money remaining. With this money, the product manufacturer purchases an option on the equity index to be tracked (this could be a market index, such as the Dow Jones, FTSE-100 or ISEQ, or a sector index, such as European pharmaceuticals, American financials or Japanese property stocks) and the participation rate will be dependent upon the option provider's view of the market chosen.
- An option, again despite many people's belief, is a relatively simple concept. Assuming the higher number of £20,968.55 in the example, what the product manufacturer wants to know is how much this figure can buy in the index/indices chosen – this

will dictate the tracker's 'participation rate'. The £20,968.55 will be paid immediately to the option provider, who will promise to sell a certain amount of the index being tracked, at today's price (or, to be exact, at the price on the 'strike date' of the tracker, the effective start date of the six-year term in this example). So, to get a participation rate of 100%, the £20,968.55 would have to secure £100,000 worth of the index, at today's price, six years from now.

- The two elements come together at the end of the tracker period. If the index is more valuable in six years' time than it was on the start date, then the option will be exercised and profit will be made. In this example, for simplicity, I'm going to assume that the index being tracked is valued at 1,000 on the start date and has grown to 2,000 in the six years. As the deposit account matures (at £100,000) within the tracker, under the terms of the option, that £100,000 can buy the index at 1,000 and immediately sell it the same day at 2,000, doubling the money in a day and repaying the investor £200,000 as a maturity value. However, in the event that the index being tracked has fallen in value to 750, over the six years, then the option is useless and the investor only receives the £100,000 back. In effect, the £20,968.55 paid to the option provider has been completely lost and has been replaced in the investor's hands by the guaranteed returns on the deposit element.

OK, that might not be entirely simple, but I hope that, even if it means reading it a couple of times, you get the broad picture. A tracker uses two financial products bolted together to allow an investor to get the potential returns offered by the stock market, while having a guarantee on the capital invested. In brief, your capital is ring fenced and your losses can be no lower than the money you invested in the first place.

The fact that a capital guarantee was introduced by the tracker products opened the door to investors to borrow the money to invest. In the example, the investor could happily borrow the £100,000 and invest in the tracker, as they are guaranteed to get the £100,000 back in six years' time and so are guaranteed to repay the amount borrowed at the end of the loan term. They could offer the tracker as security to the lender. This means that, from a financial underwriting point of view, the lender has a 100% guarantee on the capital. The lender's only concern when underwriting the investor's loan application is his ability to service the interest payments. From the investor's point of view, the monthly interest payments are their only concern too – and that's their only risk! Assuming, for example, no growth whatsoever in the index being tracked, at the end of six years the maximum loss the investor could suffer is the interest payments made over the six years.

By using one of the tricks of the rich, you too can increase the potential of your investment to make profit and thereby give yourself a real opportunity of financial security in the future. Another advantage this trick of the rich gives you is the ability to invest £100,000 towards your financial future, without actually having the £100,000 yourself.

Now that you understand the concept, you will be able to take advantage of this type of planning as long as capital-guaranteed tracker products are available. The borrowing and investment do not have to be arranged within one product, since you can do them separately. If you have even more appetite for risk, there are other options available, but it's beyond the scope of this book to delve too deeply into specialist investments.

So, borrowing is good, but borrow like the rich

What you've seen in this chapter is that often what we believe about money is not actually true and that those who believe in living life on the basis of 'Neither a borrower nor a lender be' will find it all but impossible to reach any form of true financial security. Borrowing to create wealth is generally a good idea, but remember to borrow in a manner that suits *your* profit agenda and run your calculations in advance. This will ensure that any foreseeable event will not result in you being forced out of the investment.

those who believe in living life on the basis of 'Neither a borrower nor a lender be' will find it all but impossible to reach any form of true financial security

Borrowing is certainly one of the tricks of the rich and I want you to learn it. The main reasons are:

- You put yourself in the way of making money with other people's money.
- As long as the return on the investment is greater than the cost of your debt, you are making money for free!
- While there are risks, it is quite likely that they are far less than you perceive them to be and you should not let fear of losing control your decision-making process. The rich don't.
- Many of the risks can be lowered by prudent planning. Making such investments inside a private retirement fund, for example, means that the true cost of the debt can be reduced by reducing the tax you pay. Fixing interest rates can remove the risk of rising costs of debt. Back testing the market you are considering for investment will let you know the type of returns that have been achieved in the past and the economic environment in which those returns were achieved. Product sellers should be able to give you historical figures for the markets you are considering and explain how and why they believe such markets will be profitable to you in the future. Such information will help with your risk analysis and may prove that, other than in a catastrophic economic environment, it is all but impossible for you not to make money.

- Finally, you are likely to have enjoyed considerable wealth creation through this method before, without necessarily thinking about it. Many home-owners have experienced massive increases in their property values on homes they bought with 90%+ debt attached, even when recent property devaluation is taken into account. I suggest that the vast bulk of the wealth created has been due to the debt (because you personally did not have to stump up the cash to buy your house); considerably more than was created by the property.

Chapter 6

Invest like the rich. What investments you should make

We're now going to look at the issues the rich take into account as they decide whether a particular investment is right for them. You too can learn these tricks and you'll find making an investment decision as easy as the rich find it.

Risk

Before looking at the different investment classes, let's spend some time discussing investment risk. Financial freedom cannot be achieved without risks being taken, so let me make clear:

> 'There is no such thing as no risk'.

The rich know this. And it is true because we live in a world of inflation.

Historically, many people used the 'mattress' investment method, keeping their cash close at hand and not trusting anyone, either individuals or institutions, to keep their money safe. Instead, they slept on it, ensuring that, at least during the night-time hours, their money could not be stolen. Many of these people believed this meant that they could not lose money, but, of course, they were wrong.

Over the 20 years from 1990 to 2010, the average annual inflation rate in the UK has been 3.13%,[4] which means that the value of the money kept under a mattress fell by 3.13% each year. In

[4] *Source*: Central Statistics Office.

effect, 'mattressed' money lost its spending power (its real value) at an alarming rate. So if you had placed £10,000 under your mattress back in 1990 and only brought it out to the light of day in 2010, its real value would have decreased to £5,400. Or, to put it another way, the goods that could have been purchased back in 1990 for £10,000, would now cost you £18,520. These are frightening statistics.

So, you can see there is no such thing as no risk. Even cash deposits, which for the most part pay an annual interest, do so at a rate less than inflation – and so actually lose you money. Many people hold these deposits for the long term and fool themselves into thinking they are getting richer by simply looking at a slowly rising number in their bank book. What the rich know, and you need to be aware of, is that you only make money on your investments if the rate of growth you are getting exceeds the rate of inflation. Taking our earlier example, if our mattress investor

there is no such thing as no risk

had abandoned the bedroom for the bank vault and had received an average annual interest rate of 2%, then his £10,000 would have grown to £14,860 over the 20 years. However, inflation in the meantime means that his £10,000 needs to be worth £18,520 to keep the same buying power – so, in real terms, he lost £3,660.

you only make money on your investments if the rate of growth you are getting exceeds the rate of inflation

So what can you learn from this?

- **There is no such thing as an investment with no risk**. This does not mean, I am afraid, that certain product sellers will not try to sell you investments which they claim are no-risk; there is always a risk. You've probably heard the phrase, 'If it seems too good to be true, it probably is.' This is certainly a good attitude to cultivate as you enter the investment arena.
- **No matter how much your future investments return on an annual basis, if the return is not beating the inflation rate, then you are losing money!** Any investment you consider in the future needs to prove to you its ability to out-perform the expected inflation rate. When examining future investments, the rich are *only* interested in what is known as the 'real yield', that is the yield *above* the rate of inflation.

I want to look a little more closely at what you can do, to invest well, to beat inflation. We'll consider the various things you can invest in – these are known as 'investment classes', and we'll see how you can apply the tricks of the rich so as to judge them for yourself. We will start with the favourite investment of people worldwide: property.

Property

There are two main types of property investment:

- residential
- commercial (retail/office/warehouses).

Each type has different forces at work and different prospects for future growth. I'm not expecting you to become a property expert overnight, and I am sure that most rich people investing in property are not experts either, but they do know the questions to ask and the dangers that can be encountered.

Residential property

Firstly, let's look at the residential market – a market which for many – though not all – has produced huge returns over the last two decades. What forces are at work in this market and what tricks do you need to consider when deciding whether property investing, and property rental, offer substantial opportunities for you to make money?

Firstly, **interest rates**. Let's look at why they matter, where they are now and, most importantly, where they are going in the foreseeable future. Interest rates are important for two reasons:

- **They will dictate how much you pay for your loan.** We know that interest rates are the cost to you, paid to the lender – usually your bank or building society – for them providing the money. Obviously, as interest rates rise, the cost of debt rises and so the viability of any property you might purchase can be affected. I know we have dealt with this topic earlier but it is vitally important that you develop the habits of the rich and so the following points bear repeating:
    - Often, when considering a particular property, the rich will 'stress test' the deal, asking how much the loan will cost if rates rise by 1% or 2% per annum. Based on the assumed

rental income of the particular property being considered, this allows you predict how much of your own money might be demanded from the investment.

- Remember too to assume only 10 months a year letting. There will be times when your property is empty for repairs and/or as one tenant leaves to be replaced by another. Assuming a month or two each year without rental is a good discipline to impose on yourself.

- **As rates rise and the cost of finance increases, potential buyers are priced out of the market**. For example, some who could afford to buy your property (when you come to sell) when interest rates stand at 3% per annum may not be able to afford it if rates rise to 4% per annum and so rising rates limit the number of potential buyers out there. So long-term rises in interest rates can remove many buyers from the marketplace, reducing competition for your property and possibly even reducing its capital value.

The trick of the rich is to do your maths properly at the start and, where possible, to use either the interest-only or the retirement-backed loan repayment methods detailed earlier.

> the trick of the rich is to do your maths properly at the start

Bear in mind that all you can influence are the *costs* of the investment. The future value (and your profit) will be dictated by the marketplace. This is the reason the rich take such care and attention when making a purchase and use their knowledge to negotiate the very best deal they can.

Another trick is to raise your finance before you go looking for the property. All too often, newcomers to the property investment market rush out, filled with enthusiasm, find the 'perfect' property and then have only a short time to raise the loan and close the deal. Acting in this way lets the bank hold all the cards.

With a deadline in place, you're going to be more concerned about whether you'll lose the property to someone else, or if you're going to get the money in time. Because of this, it's tempting to be less concerned about the cost and structure of the loan itself.

You should approach a lender before you start looking so that you can get what is termed 'approval in principle'. This means that, before you look at a property at all, you know exactly how much you can borrow and how much it will cost – and, since there is no immediate urgency on your part, you have time to 'haggle' over price and structure. Don't be afraid to do what the rich do: approach a number of banks and create competition for your business – this can only lead to an improved deal for you. If you have no time to do all of this yourself, don't hesitate to hire an adviser, as long as he is fee-based (that is, he works for you, not for a lender or a group of lenders) and can offer impartial advice. As we've already seen in *Tricks of the Rich*, a good fee-based adviser will save you much more in the longer term than they will cost.

a good fee-based adviser will save you much more in the longer term than they will cost

Remember, as long as your property investment can be relatively painless (in other words, the maths show that, within reasonable assumptions, it is affordable), then it is of little importance what the value is tomorrow or even next year. It is the value on the day you sell that is important – and the day you might plan to sell is the day you have set in the future to reach financial freedom. Over any long-term period in modern history, property has always increased in value and, as long as you have the time to wait, it is all but assured that history will repeat itself. Aiming for financial freedom is not a 'get rich quick scheme', it is applying the tricks of the rich to your own circumstances in order, over time, to attain and, just as important, to maintain complete financial independence.

Commercial property

Interest rates, as well as the rental yields (the income you'll receive from renting something out), influence the value of these properties, so the comments made in the residential section also apply to commercial property.

However, in practice, the real guide to commercial property valuations is the rents they command. Again, as you consider this type of investment, well-prepared maths should be your true guide. If you are buying a new property, or one without a tenant in place, ask the agent for proof of rents on similar properties in the area. Several examples – certainly more than one – are ideal. Base your calculations on the lowest rent figure. This way, it's more likely that any surprises you receive on the rent are positive, not negative.

> the real guide to commercial property valuations is the rents they command

Spend some time in the area you are targeting; see where it is busy and where it is not. If you are considering a shop, look at all other shops in the area and the businesses occupying them. Are they brand-name businesses? If not, it's likely that your future tenant will be a small business rather than a national or multi-national. This, of course, increases your risk and you will want to be convinced that this increased risk is reflected in the price you are being asked to pay.

If you are considering an office, look at the other offices in the locality and identify what type of businesses occupy them. Do not forget about planning regulations. Make sure the premises meets all of them (health and safety, fire, disabled access). It is not uncommon for older offices to be sold on without meeting up-to-date regulations.

If you are buying a property with an existing tenant, make sure there is enough time left on the lease before you pay a premium for a property with a guaranteed, immediate, cash flow. The financial strength of the tenant, the length of time left on the lease, and the current level of rent, will all contribute to the price.

No matter what type of property you decide on, unless you are an expert yourself, hire a professional surveyor to give it the once-over. Make sure the surveyor knows the planning and other regulations applicable to the property and views it with those in mind. Finally, check the rent history of your chosen area. In the last few years, have rents been going up or down? Written evidence should be sought if this information is being supplied by the seller and, whichever way rents have been going, ask the agent why, if at all, he thinks things will improve, stay as they are or get worse over time.

no matter what type of property you decide on, hire a professional surveyor to give it the once-over

The ideal property, of course, is one where the rental income will repay the entire cost of your loan as well as achieving good capital growth (that is, the property grows in value too). However, such a property is very hard to find. Even if you can find one, they tend to be in areas that depend on urban renewal schemes for growth in property values, which substantially increases the risk. Many areas (such as Manchester for the Commonwealth Games in 2002, east London for the Olympics in 2012, Glasgow for the 2014 Commonwealth Games) have seen urban renewal in the last 20 years or so, and as this redevelopment continues, it is very probable that areas considered 'poorer' today will become more and more popular and, with that, more and more valuable in years to come – but this is not guaranteed. If you buy in these areas and plans for redevelopment are in place and available from local authorities, while you may face some tenancy problems or even security problems in the short term, as long as the redevelopment takes place, you will also get substantial growth. The question for you is whether you can live with the risks involved. If you cannot, buy somewhere else.

Stocks and shares

In my experience, most people have a somewhat irrational fear of the stock market. They will concentrate on the various crashes that world markets have suffered over the years. They will use the horror stories that came out of those crashes as legitimate reasons for not investing and will proudly pat themselves on the back for their decision to stay away from this investment medium.

The rich know something that the rest of us don't: a property boom is *only* possible if the world's stock markets are rising; everything is linked. Property rises in price when there are more and more buyers seeking property, and there are only more and more buyers when people are doing well financially. Generally speaking, these people are 'doing well' because they have successful careers and they only have successful careers when their employers are paying them well, which in turn is linked to the success of the business. So, as you can see, property prices are inextricably linked to the stock markets and *only* rise when the market is rising.

a property boom is *only* possible if the world's stock markets are rising

While it is true that there are specific examples that prove otherwise (either a particular property has enjoyed 'super' growth and outperformed the stock markets, or a particular stock did not rise in value as expected), this perfectly illustrates the second point I want to make about stock market investment. When investing in the stock markets, it pays to have as broad a portfolio as possible. Because you'll get exposure to a wide variety of stocks, it dilutes the risk you take: the danger in investing lies in simply pinning all your hopes on one particular stock. Different types of companies do better or worse at different times of the economic cycle and

when investing in the stock markets, it pays to have as broad a portfolio as possible having exposure to a wide range of companies in different sectors should mean that, at any given time (other than in a market crash situation), at least some of your holdings are rising in value.

> the way you invest in these markets will impact on how profitable those investments will be

The trick is to learn that the way you invest in these markets will also impact on how profitable those investments will be. Below are my suggestions for some that would be good to think about, with my comments on each.

Pooled investment funds

There is a multitude of what are known as 'equity funds' on offer from insurance companies, investment banks and other fund manager groups. An equity fund is one that exclusively invests in the stock markets – some offer exposure to many markets at once, others are more specific in the markets they target.

The benefits of these types of funds are easy to see:

- First, they offer the diversification I discussed earlier. They hold many stocks and allow access to the private investor for relatively small amounts (the usual minimum investment is around £3,000).
- Second, they offer some degree of expertise, as the fund manager makes the buy and sell decisions on your behalf.

The drawback to these funds is the costs, which can be so high that the potential for your investments to achieve the growth they deserve is all but eliminated from the start. These costs can include:

- up to 3.5% of your investment amount paid in commission to the product-seller (while commission rates range between 0% and 3.5%, typically these products are sold at top commission rates)

- up to an additional 5% taken by the insurance company or bank as you enter the fund (commonly known as the bid/offer spread)
- an annual management fee levied by the fund manager, which can be up to 1.8% per annum.

This means that you can lose up to 8.5% of your investment on the day you make it, and up to a further 1.8% of each year's growth after that. You need strong performance from the stock markets to make up for these charges!

A further drawback can be the manager himself – the rich know that it is people, not institutions, who manage money. You need to find out, in advance of any decision, how the manager has performed in the past – so insist on seeing historical performance figures for the fund. Also, even when the history looks good, be sure that the people who produced these historical figures are still employed by the particular company. I have seen some companies that use excellent historical returns to win new business, when the people who delivered the excellent performance have long since moved on.

> the rich know that it is people, not institutions, who manage money

Finally, pay little or no attention to the league tables that appear periodically in the financial press. They are often worse than useless, and cannot be used to justify any investment decision. I say this for two reasons:

- Many such league tables illustrate gross returns. They take no account of the charges levied on the funds.
- They can illustrate performance achieved by different people from those currently managing the fund.

Exchange traded funds

ETFs are relatively new and offer private investors a viable alternative to the pooled funds. They are, in effect, trackers – investment vehicles that track the performance of different markets (you can buy an ETF to track the US, UK, European, etc, markets) or sectors (you can track the performance of financial, pharmaceutical, food, etc, stocks). They guarantee you will receive the performance of the market or sector being tracked. ETFs outperform most similarly positioned pooled investment funds because of their lack of charges. Even if the managers of the pooled funds simply matched the performance of the market sector in which they are interested (and many commentators will tell you that it is very rare indeed for a manager to match or outperform the index against which he is benchmarked), you will get less profit than with an ETF, as the manager's fee and all the other charges mentioned earlier have to come out of your gross return.

In an ETF, typically, the only cost you pay is a 1% charge to get in and a 1% charge to get out, with a very low annual management charge of between 0.1% and 0.5%. Compare this to the charging structure outlined for pooled funds and, simply put, more of your money reaches the investment and thus you make more profit.

Remember a useful trick of the rich: pay as little in charges as you possibly can.

remember a useful trick of the rich: pay as little in charges as you possibly can

Buying shares directly – direct equity purchase

If you recall, earlier in this chapter we considered the need to limit your risk by having diverse investments. But the first problem that any investor (except for the super-rich) faces is that to get the diversification needed to dilute risk, it requires much more money than most of us have at our disposal. Most stockbrokers (people paid on commission to sell stocks and shares) have a minimum 'deal' limit of around £1,000, which means that they will not sell you less than £1,000 worth of a particular stock. To get the type of investment diversification that either pooled investment funds or ETFs can deliver (for minimum amounts of £3,000 and £1,000 respectively), an individual investor would need to invest between £70,000 and £100,000.

This inability to get the broad exposure that dilutes risk means that investing directly in the stock markets is usually a good deal riskier, since the average investor can only afford to invest in one or two stocks. With additional risk comes additional potential for both reward and loss, but I would still advise you if you're new to this, to use one of the other two methods I've outlined earlier.

Stockbrokers will argue that, with good advice and guidance from them, the rewards will be higher; however, I seriously doubt that. Remember, these people are not advisers, they are product-sellers, paid on commission (payable, by the way, whether you are buying or selling) to sell you shares, so it is worthwhile having an attitude of: 'Well, they would say that, wouldn't they?' If you are hell-bent on owning stocks directly, then be sure to ask for a comparison of the performance of the stockbroker's market portfolio against the market in general and their competitors' versions. If they cannot or will not give you this, walk away. There is only one reason why they won't share this information – their performance is bad.

allowing the broker to decide when to buy and sell shares for you would be like handing over control of the asylum to the lunatics

If you do open a dealing account, make it an 'advisory' account – one where every transaction has to be approved directly by you. Do not go for the alternative – a 'discretionary' account. This gives away complete control of your account, allowing the broker to decide when to buy and sell shares for you and, as they make a commission every time they buy or sell, it would be like handing over control of the asylum to the lunatics.

However, if you do not want the bother of having to make ongoing decisions about your stock portfolio, invest via one of the other methods described earlier, particularly the ETF. You will pay far less in fees, take less risk and are more likely to get a better return than any fund manager or stockbroker could deliver.

Private equity

Investment in a business venture does not have to be made via the stock markets; it can be done directly. There are many start-up businesses out there looking for investors and this is a legitimate option for any investor. Of course, like any investment, it comes with risks attached – greater risks than you face in the mature stock markets. However, as we've already seen, with greater risk comes the potential of greater reward, which can be spectacular. A friend of mine started his own business nine years ago with £12,500 of his own money. His stake today is valued at around £1,200,000 - an annual yield or return of 66%. So you can see there is potential in the private equity market: like the rich, you simply have to know how to judge the opportunity and, of course, where to find it.

Where the latter is concerned, you may know someone who has a good idea and is about to start up, or someone who has already started but could do with a cash investment. If not, take a look at the classified advertisements in your local or national newspapers. These regularly contain advertisements from businesspeople looking for partners with cash to invest. At the same time, talk to whoever can help source an investment opportunity – accountants, venture capitalist funds or others – and get the word out that you have money and are looking for a suitable investment opportunity.

When you identify a potential investment, be sure to ask the correct questions. I have listed below what the rich believe to be three of the most important:

- **What do the financial projections look like?** As a bank manager said to me, 'There is no such thing as a bad set of projections' – something to bear in mind as you view any set of figures in the future. Question the projections. Why does the promoter (the person looking for your money) believe that the sales and profits illustrated can be achieved? What other, preferably independent, evidence can he show you to back up the figures?

Question the projections

- **How much of the promoter's own money is being invested?** I cannot tell you how many times I have sat down with promoters of one business idea or another who want to risk my money and not their own. Finding out how much of his own money is involved in the project is imperative and tells you two things:
  - It is a good indication of the promoter's real belief in the potential of the project. If he is unwilling to risk his own money, my advice, in the vast majority of cases, would be not to risk yours.
  - It offers an insight into the promoter's own financial situation. Perhaps he does not have the money to invest and this, in and of itself, is not a reason to dismiss the idea. However, it does raise the question, 'How much of this new business's income is being paid to the promoter?' I suggest that such income should be at a minimum, otherwise your goal (making profit) and the promoter's may not be aligned. Suggest a basic income for the promoter, with some form of profit share being introduced to bring his income up to a reasonable level. This will mean he is just as interested in making profit as you are and should do everything in his power to drive the business into profit quickly.
- **How will you get your money back?** Finally, always look for an exit mechanism – how and when are you going to get your money, including your gains, back? Insist on an exit mechanism being part of the up-front agreement. There is no point trying to negotiate after your money has gone into the project. Remember, a minority share in a private limited company is only worth what the majority shareholder will pay for it – there

are usually few other buyers. This is why you want, not only a pre-agreed way of leaving, but also a pre-agreed valuation process. Otherwise, you may leave yourself at the mercy of the promoter. Last, but by no means least, satisfy yourself that the promoter, based on the growth assumptions in the business plan, will have the financial ability to buy you out at the pre-agreed time. Assets tied up in small businesses, with no ability to turn them into cash, are less than guaranteed.

a minority share in a private limited company is only worth what the majority shareholder will pay for it

Other ways of investing

There are, of course, many other ways to get exposure to equities, which, historically, have been the most successful investment assets. However, it is beyond the scope of this book to outline them all, so I've chosen the most common methods and I hope the guidance given here ensures that your investments in the future will reap the rewards they deserve.

Government and corporate bonds

Government or corporate bonds (called 'gilts', because the original certificates were edged in gold) are, in effect, a loan by you to the government, company or individual issuing the bond. You give them your money, usually for a fixed period of time, and in exchange they guarantee to pay you a certain rate of interest for the term and give you back your capital (the loan) at the end.

these are often much closer to deposit accounts than they are to stocks and shares

From a risk profile point of view, these vehicles are often much closer to deposit accounts than they are to stocks and shares and can offer a reasonable alternative to deposits for the medium- to long-term (three years +) investor.

However, when looking at such vehicles, you must always bear in mind that any guarantee is only as good as the government, company or individual underwriting it. Therefore, typically you will get a higher interest rate, the more 'risky' the market perception of the bond. It is up to you to satisfy yourself as to the risk being taken and to judge for yourself whether you can take that risk. I have seen bonds with interest payments of less than 3% per annum and some as high as 16% per annum. The former is more likely to be issued by a sovereign state, for the most part making it a particularly strong guarantee, while the latter is likely to be issued by a high-risk corporation, giving it, in the jargon, 'junk bond' status.

If this is an investment type that interests you, remember it is a specialist area and requires specialist help. Use the tricks of the rich you have learned, seek out a real financial adviser – one who will sell you advice, not one only interested in selling you a bond – and tread carefully. Always remember, all guarantees are *not* the same, and the less risk you are willing to take, the less interest you are likely to receive.

Cash deposits

I do not consider cash deposits an investment type. I see them more as a place where those who are too afraid to invest their money 'keep it safe'. As such, in my mind, the cash deposit is the modern-day mattress, although this time we have choices as to which mattress to use.

the cash deposit is the modern-day mattress

These accounts have two main uses: firstly, to house your 'emergency fund'. It is generally recommended that you keep approximately six months' lifestyle income on short-term deposit. This is *not* an investment decision, but a practical one. As you travel towards financial freedom and make the longer-term investments that are going to take you there, you want to protect that process as much as possible. Having six months' income available at a moment's notice means that, in the event of a mini cash crisis (it might be a short-term illness – yours or a relative's; the need to replace a car or other item of importance; the chance of a lifetime to travel to a far-flung destination, etc), your journey to financial freedom will not be interrupted.

But should you spend this money? What would the rich do?

My grandfather used to say, 'Treat every day like it is your last, because one day you'll be right' and I'm very fond of this saying. There are some people who will tell you that, until financial freedom is achieved, you should live a life of self-denial, but I do not belong to this school of thought. You must spend some of your money on enjoying life – otherwise, you simply end up as a rich corpse. However, I do believe that you should be aware of the true costs of these frivolous moments and that you should make your decisions armed with a knowledge of these costs. (If you have forgotten the real costs, please reread the *Consumer debt* section of Chapter 3.)

you must spend some of your money on enjoying life – otherwise, you simply end up as a rich corpse

The second use for cash deposits is a short-term holding position in advance of making a longer-term investment decision. When using them for this purpose, do not forget to shop around, compare rates and haggle. It is your money and you deserve to have it work as hard for you as possible.

If, despite my advice, you are going to use long-term deposit accounts as an investment vehicle, then do not be too optimistic about their future performance. Committing for longer terms will generally improve the interest rates you receive, but you should only expect such products at best to maintain the real value of your cash – however, generally, you will have to commit your money for two to three years to have any chance of receiving a return that matches or outpaces inflation.

If using money is like football, then people 'investing' in deposits are sitting in the stand watching the game. Those on the pitch are playing the game, making longer-term investments in real assets, taking the calculated risks necessary to become financially free. If you are happy to be a spectator, or if your circumstances are such that you simply cannot take any risk, then so be it, stick with your cash deposits. However, as you do so, for your own mental health – if nothing else – leave behind your aspirations of wealth and true financial security, because they will only ever be a pipe dream. Continuing the football analogy for a moment, the spectator in the stand is fooling himself if they yearn for the elation the player feels when the game is won, while they stay firmly seated on the sidelines. A spectator can never experience that elation, no matter how much they want it.

Chapter 7

The rich keep more of their income and how you can too

The rich realise that *how* they earn their money plays a very important role as they strive to reach and maintain financial freedom. Of course, it is not within everyone's capacity to dictate the manner in which their income is earned, especially if they are an employee paid via the PAYE system. While I will return to the PAYE earner later in this chapter, I want to first concentrate on the self-employed.

The benefits of being self-employed

The rich earn most of their income through a private limited company – for the following reasons:

- Limited liability is a superb protection for the business owner. The limited company structure allows you to limit the financial risks you are taking to the amount of capital (sometimes referred to as shareholder funds) you have invested in the business. Compare this to the alternative, known as the sole trader (or partnership, if there is more than one proprietor) structure. If you trade this way, there is no legal difference between you and your business and in the event of a business failure, you are completely responsible. What this means is that you personally owe every penny your business owes and could lose everything – including your home, your investments and even your retirement funds.

limited liability is a superb protection for the business owner

- As discussed earlier, retirement allowances will play a huge role in your journey to financial freedom. They offer the most accessible tax concessions, allowing you to invest money before you pay tax (*Golden Rule No. 2*). The simple fact is that retirement allowances are considerably higher for a proprietary director of a private limited company than for a sole trader. While the caps on retirement funds are the same for personally funded pensions as they are for those funded via a limited company, funding via a limited company can allow you to accumulate the maximum cap far more quickly.

retirement allowances will play a huge role in your journey to financial freedom

- Earning income through a private limited company means that income arrives to you without tax interference. Unlike the PAYE worker, whose income is taxed before he even sees it, a limited company bills for its services, gets paid and does not have to pay tax on its income until six months after the end of its financial year. Not only this, but on any profit made within the company, current corporation tax rates in the UK are levied at between 21% and 28%, a significant saving when compared to the maximum combined income tax and National Insurance levies rates paid by the sole trader.

  This six-month delay in payment of taxation gives you an opportunity for tax planning – time that most workers (who have tax deducted before they see their income) simply do not have. Proper use of retirement allowances (and you'll need help here from an impartial, fee-charging adviser) will allow you to keep a lot more of the income you generate, and dovetailing this planning procedure with other tax planning structures can help you keep even more. The lower levels of corporation tax also mean the business itself can keep more of its income, allowing you to plough money back into the business and make it a bigger and more profitable entity.

So, here are the three excellent reasons why the rich, when at all possible, operate their commercial activity through a private limited company.

- It helps to keep much more of the income being generated.
- It gives an opportunity to build a bigger and more profitable business.
- It reduces substantially the risks being taken.

By ensuring that they concentrate on *all* aspects of their financial lives – in this case, on the legal structure used to earn their income – the rich ensure they minimise the **risks** being taken and the **taxes** being paid.

I cannot think of one reason why anyone – other than some business activities that cannot do so under either legislative or professional association rules – would operate as a sole trader, and yet there are many, many sole traders out there. Why?

I cannot think of one reason why anyone would operate as a sole trader

This is a question that has bothered me for some time and I have posed it to many clients and their accountants (in my experience, the accountant is usually involved in the decision to act as a sole trader). I have yet to receive a satisfactory reply. When I come across a situation like this, my cynical side prompts me to ask, 'If the client does not benefit from the sole trader environment, does anyone?'

In my opinion, the accountant benefits in that he does not carry the same financial liability when producing accounts for a sole trader as when producing audits for a private limited company. So, while the fee for a set of sole trader accounts is typically that bit lower than the equivalent fee for a limited company, the accountant is taking more risk for the slightly higher payment – perhaps not a sensible choice for the accountant.

So, is an accountant's advice to operate in a sole trader environment purely to the benefit of the accountant? I cannot answer this question, but if you are operating as a sole trader now, it is a question you need to ask. Of course, posing it as I have done here may aggravate, if not insult, your accountant. Instead, ask him for a list of reasons why you should continue as a sole trader and why you should not switch to a private limited company structure. Ask him to provide this list in writing, as putting advice in writing concentrates the mind, and then come to your own conclusions. As I have already stated, I have never heard an argument for the sole trader environment that even comes close to any one of the arguments for the private limited company alternative.

Not everyone can dictate how they earn their money but there are many sole traders reading this who now can. Remember, at the start of this book I mentioned that, to reach the goal of financial freedom, you would have to change the way you think about money and the actions you take in connection with your money. So, if you are self-employed and you are a sole trader, resolve today to take action. Call your accountant at the earliest possible moment, and arrange an appointment. Even bring this book with you and let him read this passage and seek his reaction. Then ask for the list of reasons why you should continue as a sole trader and get them in writing on headed paper. In Ireland, IFSRA (the Irish Financial Services Regulatory Authority), the entity charged with protecting the public against improper financial advice, has a maxim when it comes to such advice: 'If it is not in writing, it does not exist.' Insisting that any financial advice offered to you is confirmed in writing, and on the headed paper of the adviser, protects you into the future. If you follow that advice and, later, it can be shown that the adviser was negligent in issuing it, then you have the right and, with the advice confirmed in writing on headed paper, the proof to sue for the losses you suffered.

Ensuring that you incorporate this *trick of the rich* in your own financial world will mean that you are provided with all the information required for you to make the best financial decision possible.

I pay tax before I see my money. What would the rich do?

Become self-employed

There will also be PAYE workers reading this who may have an opportunity to switch to the self-employed environment via their own private limited company. In the recent past, this has been something that people working in the IT industry have made use of. Many programmers and analysts now operate as contractors, providing their services on short-term contracts through their own companies.

And, believe it or not, there could be advantages for the employers here too. If it is possible for you to switch to this structure, there are obvious savings for the employer – for example, since the contractor is now self-employed, the employer need not provide pension benefits, health insurance or any of the other ancillary benefits offered to employees.

If you are reading this as an employee, you will no doubt see that there is much to sacrifice if you move to your own private limited company. However, as with the sole trader earlier, the benefits you'll reap, in terms of your ability to actually reach financial freedom, far outweigh those sacrifices. Certainly, there are risks, but by now, as you come to think more and more like the rich, the existence of risks should not surprise you. Yes, you will have to pay for your own health insurance and other ancillary benefits, but do not fool yourself; you already pay for them, as your employer takes such payments into account when negotiating your salary. Finally, yes, you will have to fund your own retirement benefits and this you will do via the self-administered pension fund explained in Chapter 4. Remember, once you reach financial freedom, you will not need a pension in the same way as others do – it will simply be one of your assets that provides the complete financial security that financial freedom brings.

Stay in your job

For those employees who are unable to make the leap into the realm of self-employment – whether because you simply cannot bring yourself to take the risks involved or your employer flatly refuses the contractor relationship – all is not lost. There is an investment product for sale in the marketplace known as an additional voluntary contribution (AVC) scheme that allows you to keep more of the money you earn. This product, which is usually available alongside your main superannuation (pension) scheme, allows you to invest a certain amount of your income before you pay tax.

So, for example, taking the same retirement allowance of £3,600 as used in Chapter 2, you could elect to have this amount of your income diverted to your AVC scheme. This money is deducted from your income before tax or National Insurance levies are calculated, giving you an immediate tax saving in the UK of between 20% and 50%, depending upon whether you pay the lower or higher tax rate.

Example 6

The power of AVCs

Caroline earns £40,000 a year before tax, taking home around £26,500 after tax and deductions. Of this £26,500, she invests around £200 per month (£2,400 per annum) into a pooled investment fund. She is prepared to make the sacrifices (and take the risks) necessary for wealth accumulation. However, paying attention to Golden Rule No. 2 will substantially improve her ability to create wealth.

Caroline should elect to pay an additional voluntary contribution (AVC) of £300 a month (£3,600 a year). This payment, which will come out of her gross income (before tax and National Insurance deductions), will cost circa £200 from take-home pay (assuming the maximum tax relief), so in spending power nothing has changed. But she has moved from saving £200 per month to saving £300 per month, with the extra £100 being supplied by the taxman.

Not only is Caroline getting an additional 50% into her savings scheme, but also the returns made within the scheme are now tax-free. Getting to keep more of the money you earn simply makes you wealthier!

'So, where's the catch?', I hear you ask – and there is a small catch: you cannot access your savings until you reach retirement. However, that may be earlier than you think. You need to check the retirement rules for your occupation, but this could be as early as 50. This 'catch' applies to all the retirement planning vehicles mentioned, with the earlier access age often applying to those employed by companies (employees may require the approval of their employer to gain access before the normal retirement age, while proprietary directors can, within the rules, gain access at their own discretion) and the later age to sole traders (another reason to move to a private limited company structure).

However, I do not see the lack of access as a drawback. I see it as an important tool to be used as you strive to reach financial freedom. Many of you reading this book will have been earning good income for many years and yet what have you managed to accumulate over that time? If you are like most people I meet, at best you will have a home in which you enjoy some equity (so you owe your lender less than the house is worth) and a whole bunch of liabilities that have been used to fund the purchase of your car, your spouse's car, your new kitchen ... etc. The simple fact is that if you can spend your

> the simple fact is that if you can spend your savings, you will

savings, you will (and may I suggest that you have done it before), so having a legislative barrier to spending the money is actually a benefit rather than a disadvantage.

Remember to change the way you think

I have mentioned repeatedly that, if you truly wish to achieve financial freedom, you must change the way you think and act with regard to money. This is a key change: saving tax is a futile exercise if all you do is spend the savings on more 'stuff'. You have to demonstrate a new-found discipline to set money aside, to work for you rather than you working for it.

if you truly wish to achieve financial freedom, you must change the way you think and act with regard to money

Summary

I have said this before, but it bears repeating, I think: it is the **costs** that you pay as you earn and invest money that will ultimately dictate the financial future that awaits you. The greatest cost for all of us who live in the western world is **tax** and the rich have realised that the amount of tax to be paid is dictated as much by *how* the income is earned as by how much income is earned.

While there is a reduction in risk if you can change from sole trader to limited liability, the huge potential savings are in taxation. This means that, if it is at all possible, you should earn your money through your own private limited company. It simply multiplies your opportunities for effective tax planning. Although there is a price to pay for some of the tax benefits hinted at here, in that you cannot *spend* the money until later, the rich also recognise that money that is available for spending is spent and financial security cannot be provided by that type of savings. A regulatory barrier to spending the money is a way of ensuring that the temptation to spend the money is removed from the outset, and so the money is guaranteed to be available when needed. If you cannot change the way you earn your money, then you need to change the way you save your money, and taking advantage of personal pension allowances is the best place to start.

The next chapter deals with other methods that can be used to reduce taxation, but one word of caution – do not use these methods until you have taken maximum advantage of retirement allowances *first*! It never ceases to amaze me when I meet new clients who have invested in numerous tax schemes and yet have consistently ignored their retirement allowances. Do not forget, tax schemes are also financial products sold by agents to generate commission for them. As such, they are not to be entered into lightly and I generally recommend that you act like the rich and seek impartial advice before getting involved. There is little doubt that, typically, tax schemes represent substantially greater risk than any regular retirement plan and, often, the tax break is not absolutely guaranteed.

Chapter 8

How the rich pay less tax

As we've seen in earlier chapters, investing your money before you pay tax will make you immediately wealthier, simply by allowing you to *keep* more of what you earn. The fact that retirement funds not only provide this tax concession, but that they are also exempt from many ongoing taxes, means they provide a double benefit. This is why I suggest that you use these allowances first, and only look for other ways of saving tax once you are at your maximum. Of course, I am not for a moment suggesting that you fail to identify other opportunities to save tax, just be sure to use those that are guaranteed, before moving on.

Tax incentive schemes

Tax incentives are generally offered by the government – either at local or national level – and are typically designed to attract capital investment. In my home country of Ireland I have seen tax incentive schemes that cover activities as diverse as the making of Hollywood movies and the redevelopment of run-down inner-city areas. From the government's point of view, they are designed to achieve a number of different benefits. In these two Irish examples, the first tax scheme mentioned brought a new (and very rich) business to our shores, creating jobs, tax receipts and a window into Ireland which immeasurably bolstered tourism. The second ensured the private sector went a long way to solving a growing social problem, while at the same time purchasing land that allowed more modern homes to be built (albeit in more suburban areas) for many disadvantaged families.

I wanted to point out the benefits enjoyed by the state in these examples, because I also want to dispel a myth. In Ireland, and, in a much more limited way, in other jurisdictions, I have often read media articles that present tax-incentive schemes in a very simplistic 'the rich getting richer while the poor are getting poorer' manner. Rarely, if ever, have I read anything in a daily newspaper that promotes the benefits of such schemes. This has coloured many people's opinion of these incentives, to a point where they deny themselves the benefits because enjoying them would seem greedy. The myth goes that to actively seek to reduce their tax burden would mean they join the ranks of the fat cats, people making money from denying some necessity to those less fortunate. While no one can deny that tax breaks mean the rich *keep* more of the money they earn (a trick I am suggesting you should cultivate for yourself), they generally only receive the tax breaks because they have invested their own money (taking the risks those investments represent) in a manner that creates a major knock-on effect.

I realise I am labouring this point, but I believe it is important that you make your financial decisions with as much relevant information to hand as possible. Long before I understood the workings of tax incentive schemes to the extent I do now, I often spoke to clients about reducing their tax burden, only for them to refuse. Some felt what I was suggesting must be illegal, others wrongly thought they could only enjoy a benefit if someone else suffered a loss. Let me explain what I mean using the example of the inner-city Irish tax incentive scheme mentioned earlier.

An Irish example

In Ireland the investor could typically write off 85% of his investment (known as the capital allowance) against income tax. The top rate of income tax in Ireland today is 41%, so the investor would save £4,100 in tax for every £10,000 of capital allowance granted. For example, investing £100,000 would mean £85,000 in capital allowance, saving our investor £34,850 (41% of £85,000) in tax.

So, if across the entire inner-city scheme you imagine £10 billion was invested, £8.5 billion in capital allowances were granted and the 'rich' avoided £3.485 billion in income tax.

So, far we have looked at are the costs. What type of benefits might the Irish state have enjoyed?

- Over the 20 years the construction industry boomed, creating more jobs than ever before. This meant the Irish Exchequer received huge increases in both corporation tax (employers) and income tax (employees).
- When one industry grows, support industries, including leisure and entertainment, grow to meet the increasing demand of the growth sector. The Irish Exchequer enjoys more of the benefits listed above.
- The investors borrowed the money (£10 billion in our example) securing jobs in the banking sector, bolstering banking profits and further contributing to the Irish Exchequer via the banks' corporation tax.
- VAT on property in Ireland is charged at 13.5%. The sale of £10 billion worth of property would mean £1.35 billion in VAT receipts paid to the Irish Exchequer.
- Stamp duty in Ireland is paid at a minimum of 7% on all property over £125,000, and a maximum of 9% on any property over £875,000. Even if we assume stamp duty applied at just 3% on the £10 billion, this means that, in our example, the Irish Exchequer receives another £300 million.
- Much of the money now circulating because of the 'rich' people's investment ends up in the wallets and purses of the employees of the construction companies, banks, builder's merchants, bar owners and concert organisers ... etc. They go out and buy alcohol and cigarettes, cars and holiday homes, clothes etc, the sale of which all produces sales tax and/or excise duties to the Irish Exchequer.

> tax incentives benefit users and their country alike

So, what does all this mean? What it means is that tax incentives benefit users and their country (and, via the state, *all* taxpayers) alike. To avoid them out of some misplaced belief that they financially hurt your fellow citizen is merely robbing yourself of your right to pay as little tax as legitimately possible.

Make sure you claim your allowances

I firmly believe that the tax system in the western economies is fundamentally fair. This is not to say that we could not find unfair examples; people are inherently selfish and if they are presented with an opportunity to feather their own nest then, more often than not, they will do so. However, in my experience it is *only* the rich who exercise their rights to pay as little tax as legitimately possible, despite the fact that this is the right of everyone. So, learn this trick of the rich: you need to actively seek out opportunities to pay less tax and invest more money.

> learn this trick of the rich: actively seek out opportunities to pay less tax and invest more money

But it's not only people like me who encourage taxpayers to pay only the taxes they must pay. In Ireland, a special investigating committee of our parliament reported recently that Irish taxpayers routinely fail to claim up to £500 million in tax allowances each year. This led to a major advertising campaign, where the Revenue authorities actively encouraged the public to claim their rightful allowances. I have seen similar advertisements in the UK and I imagine the same is true throughout the western world. Remember to claim all that you're entitled to claim.

Figures from Ireland suggest that Irish taxpayers overpay tax by around £500 per annum (assuming these unclaimed tax concessions were uniformly spread across the workforce). Over a working lifetime of 30 to 40 years, had this tax been avoided and invested (assuming an annual return of 6% net) then Irish taxpayers are robbing themselves of circa £42,000 – £82,000 in accumulated wealth at the end of their working lives. Remember the trick: no matter where you earn your income and pay your taxes, the question is, how much more tax-efficient could you be?

What type of tax concessions may be available?

It is not possible to write a book like this and to list all the up-to-date tax concessions available in your country. Not only would there probably be far too many examples to correlate from far too many tax jurisdictions, listing them all would scarcely make for an entertaining read. Before getting into the type of tax concessions to watch out for, let me give a word of caution.

I have experienced many investors parting with hard-earned money simply because of the tax break! This is a completely understandable reaction from any individual who pays considerable amounts of tax, but is *not* the way to decide on an investment. And here is the point: as the rich know, it is an investment first and any tax concession is the icing on the cake. Tax breaks or tax refunds should only be taken into consideration if you have deemed the underlying investment to be sound. Over the years, I have seen people throw money at tax schemes, only to have the tax benefits completely eroded by an underlying asset which underperforms. I can assure you that, while paying tax can be painful, losing money is far more painful. When considering any investment offering a tax concession, judge the investment first, the type of asset you are investing in, the amount of your money you are willing to risk, how and when your money will be repaid to you and then let mathematics be your guide.

as the rich know, it is an investment first and any tax concession is the icing on the cake

Tax concessions can be applied to most of the taxes we pay, from basic income tax (remember the tax benefits of retirement funds discussed earlier) to capital gains tax, from VAT to inheritance tax and from stamp duty to corporate taxes. Concessions come in all shapes and sizes too, offering short- or long-term exemptions from some, or a mixture of the taxes for which you're liable. Tax concessions can be offered to corporations and other business structures; they can be for the exclusive use of individuals or open to all class of taxpayer.

No matter what type of tax concession you may use, they all have one objective in common; to help you *keep* more money! Schemes achieve this objective in many different ways:

- **Maximum concessions**: These schemes offer tax breaks as you invest your money and tax breaks on the investment as it makes a profit. Retirement plans are a good example of maximum concessions. Due to the tax deductibility of the investment, the real costs to the investor are substantially reduced. Also, within the investment, taxes are seriously curtailed, which means the investor gets to *keep* much more of the profit. In Chapter 3 you saw how increasing the tax efficiency of debt repayment (by using a retirement vehicle to repay capital) can massively increase your rate of wealth accumulation. The same will be true if you learn to seek out and apply all relevant tax concessions to your financial world.
- **Medium concessions**: These schemes offer tax breaks either as you invest the money or as the investment grows, but generally not both. They will, of course, offer fewer benefits than those discussed immediately above. Hence, my earlier suggestion to use all available retirement and pension allowances as these offer maximum concessions. However, they will be useful to those who still have income or capital exposed to tax even after all the safest tax concessions have been used. Tax breaks as you invest the money will lower your real costs, so you can afford to invest

more than when investing with after-tax money. The more you are able to invest, the more you are likely to gain, assuming a positive investment outcome.

- **Minimum concessions**: Schemes that I would typically place in this category provide a one-off, never-to-be-used-again, benefit as long as the taxpayer takes a particular, quite specific, action. They may be on offer to, for example, employees of one particular company when they invest a certain amount in that company's shares – these are sometimes known as share schemes or share incentive plans. Others may apply to retiring business owners as they sell business assets, still others to particular types of assets being passed from one generation to the next.

As already stated, tax concession schemes come and go and it is difficult to keep completely up-to-date. Ensure that you are on the mailing list of specialist advisers for such information.

ensure that you are on the mailing list of specialist advisers

The rich know all about tax concessions and are aware of how they change and develop. As someone now learning to take more control over your financial future, you will need to find out which benefits may exist.

The following examples are from Ireland. I offer them not to outline the particular tax schemes (after all, Irish tax schemes are of little interest to anyone living elsewhere) but to demonstrate the substantial wealth accumulation benefits they delivered to those who used them properly.

The key trick of the rich is that they are able to judge the true value of any tax concession in advance. In Ireland, many people rushed to the tax break, ignored the underlying investment, and actually lost money. You want to be sure that you approach your decision on a cost, benefit, and risk analysis. By doing so, mathematics will be your guide, leading you to a fully informed and more considered decision. I will give one example of each category of the tax concession as defined earlier, starting with a maximum concession.

Maximum concession example

In Ireland, as in the UK, most taxpayers have the option of investing at least part of their income *before* they pay tax. By effectively using retirement legislation, taxpayers can invest *more* money and because retirement funds are exempt from both income and capital gains tax, they will *keep* more of the profits too.

Let's look at how the purchase of an investment property can be made much more profitable by altering how the property is purchased. In our example, an investment property is being purchased for £250,000, with 30% of the purchase price being provided by the investor. The balance is being borrowed over 15 years at an interest rate of 5%. (This rate may be high or low, depending upon when you are reading this book; the rate itself, however, is relatively unimportant to the point I am trying to make, as I have used the same rate in both examples and the increased profits illustrated are due to the structure of the purchase *only*.) Income tax is assumed to be paid at the rate of 40%, the long-term rental yield is assumed to be 4% per annum and the property appreciates in value at 5% per annum. In 15 years' time the property will be valued at £519,732, on which our direct investor will pay 18% capital gains tax, thus keeping £471,180 after tax. The cost of this transaction to our investor is as follows:

Total cash payment up-front	£75,000
Monthly rent received	£833.34
Average income tax payable*	£ 160.23
Monthly loan repayments	£1,404.99
Monthly out-of-pocket costs	£731.88
Total out-of-pocket costs (£75,000 up front plus 180 payments of £731.88 per month)	£206,738.40
Internal rate of return on investment	7.45% per annum

*Tax is *only* payable on the rent received *less* the amount of interest payments made. This figure has been averaged over the full 15-year term.

Now to illustrate the power of a maximum tax concession: instead of purchasing with after-tax money, our more informed investor purchases the property within a retirement fund. This means that the initial cost of investing is reduced by 40% (always remembering that you cannot invest beyond the pension caps) and a lack of income tax along the way and capital gains tax as the property is sold on means even greater profits. Income tax is paid as funds are withdrawn from the pension fund; however, our interest here is in the amount of capital accumulated and available to deliver income in the future. This is the *only* interest the rich have and the *only* one you should have too.

So the £75,000 initial deposit costs just £45,000 in out-of-pocket expense as it is paid as a retirement contribution. There is no tax payable within the fund and the cost of paying the £571.65 per month (a lesser amount than the monthly servicing costs of the previous example, as the rental income is being paid to the tax-exempt retirement fund), which is now a retirement contribution, is just £342.99. The combination of tax concessions on the contribution and the lack of internal taxes produces an overall cost reduction of a little over £100,000. So, the investment now costs just £106,738.20 and returns income-producing assets of

£519,732 to the investor. What the tax concessions have done is to increase the internal rate of return (IRR) (the rate of wealth accumulation, as it were) by 77.7% to 13.24% per annum.

If our investor uses the retirement fund and invests more money (so that the net cost is still £75,000 up front and £731.88 per month, purchasing more property but keeping the future growth assumptions the same) the final accumulated wealth after all taxes would be £956,872. Comparing this to the £471,180 our investor will *keep* in the fully taxed example, income-producing assets have increased by £485,692 or by 103.08%. So, as you can see, this trick of the rich reduces taxes and increases the yield by 77.7% per annum, but the timing of the tax savings that are made, means that this increased yield turns into 103.08% more income-producing assets.

Most taxpayers have the opportunity to use substantial tax concessions if they choose to plan for their retirement. Be sure that you investigate your entitlements as soon as possible and that you do so with an impartial adviser. From time to time, there will be other tax schemes that offer maximum concessions such as these. Being a client of an impartial adviser, and/or being on the marketing lists of many such advisers, will ensure you are kept up-to-date with the various offerings that could apply to your world and so you get to save tax, and thus *keep* more of your money, at every available opportunity.

be sure that you investigate your entitlements as soon as possible

Medium concession example

One of the most popular uses of this type of scheme has been to encourage the renewal of inner-city slums or ghettos – in Ireland, our example was known as Section 23 relief. The tax break meant that the purchase price of a new-build property in certain designated areas less the site price (the cost attributable to the cost of the land on which the property was built) could be offset against the purchaser's Irish rental income. At times, similar tax relief was granted on the refurbishment costs of older, run-down, residential properties. So, for an investor with existing rental properties, the purchase of a Section 23 property could massively increase the amount of rental income he was able to keep.

Imagine an existing owner of rental property worth, say, £1 million, with taxable rental income of £30,000 per annum. If this were not a Section 23 property the investor would pay 40% income tax on this rent, keeping just £18,000 per annum – a yield of just 1.8% per annum. However, our clever and more informed investor sought out a tax break and purchased a Section 23 property for £250,000, 85% of this price being deemed tax-deductible (i.e. the site price was set at 15% of the total purchase price). Under this tax concession the investor could claim the tax deductions over the next seven years. Table 3 compares the tax payable with and without the Section 23.

Table 3 Tax payable comparison

Year	Rental income	Tax paid without Section 23	Tax paid with Section 23	Extra rental income kept by investor
1	£30,000	£12,000	Nil	£12,000
2	£30,000	£12,000	Nil	£12,000
3	£30,000	£12,000	Nil	£12,000
4	£30,000	£12,000	Nil	£12,000
5	£30,000	£12,000	Nil	£12,000
6	£30,000	£12,000	Nil	£12,000
7	£30,000	£12,000	£3,535	£8,465
Totals	£210,000	£84,000	£3,535	£80,465

Note: All figures rounded up or down to nearest £1.

Saving tax will always help your cash flow, as this table demonstrates; however, it will only make you wealthier if you invest the savings. Our sample investor could simply spend more money for each of the seven years covered by the tax exemption, but all that would do is improve his lifestyle for that period. This investor has learned that lesson and is using the tax breaks to help build long-term financial security. So the savings are invested and should they receive a 5% per annum net return, at the end of the tax concession a further £98,272 in wealth has been created.

saving tax will always help your cash flow; however, it will only make you wealthier if you invest the savings

By proactively altering *how* the current investments are taxed, more wealth is created as long as the investor has the discipline to invest the savings. Most of us deal with taxation on a reactive basis, paying our taxes when they are due and doing little or nothing to legitimately reduce our liabilities. The rich, however, deal with their taxation in advance and place the tax treatment of their investments at the centre of their decision-making process. In this example, our investor not only gets the additional wealth created by investing the tax savings, but the property is also likely to yield some growth in capital value and some additional rental income too. Enjoying these benefits simply mushrooms the investor's rate of wealth creation and the same will be true for you if you seek out local tax breaks for yourself. (Watch out though for the premium prices you may pay for tax-designated properties, they tend to be on sale at higher than normal retail prices.)

the rich place the tax treatment of their investments at the centre of their decision-making process

Minimum concession example

Even what appear to be small tax concessions can make a substantial difference. In Ireland, for example, there is a specific tax concession available to retiring owner managers as they sell or liquidate their business. This retirement relief allows an owner manager (who must qualify for the relief by owning shares and working in the business for pre-set periods of time) to sell his interest in the business for up to £645,000 and to pay no capital gains tax whatsoever. Should there be a similar concession available in your jurisdiction, this means that, based on the UK's capital gains tax rate of 18%, a fully qualifying individual saves £116,100 in taxes as they retire.

Knowing that the tax concession is available – and I have to say that, in my time as a financial adviser, few owner managers knew of this tax break – allows the owner to create an environment where it is possible to take the maximum advantage. For example, understanding that it is a personal benefit allows a clever business owner to give his spouse half the shares and a job in the business well in advance of the qualifying timeframe. This immediately *doubles* the tax concession to be enjoyed, bringing future benefits to £232,200. Once the spouse is a shareholder and employee, a retirement fund can be provided for the spouse, effectively doubling the retirement cap and saving substantial amounts of tax there too.

As you can see, what starts as a one-off, relatively modest, tax benefit (a tax saving of £116,100 for one's life work could mean a tax break of just £2,902.50 per annum if one works for 40 years) can be made considerably more beneficial by using it to its maximum and dovetailing with other tax concessions. You need to be aware of all the tax concessions that are available at any given time and the rules that qualify you to enjoy them. You also need to find out about any tax concessions to be enjoyed in the future and, where possible, you need to manipulate your financial world so that you *pay only the taxes you must pay*!

So, what's the catch?

Having written all that I have about tax concessions, you might expect me to tell you that you should use every legitimate tax scheme that comes your way, but I cannot. Generally speaking, there are risks to be identified, timescales to be judged and many other aspects of these schemes that will dictate whether you enjoy a superior benefit in the long term. First and foremost you have to be convinced of the bona fides of any scheme, in that you need to be sure that the benefits are actually going to be enjoyed. Once you have satisfactory confirmation (your new-found financial discipline now makes you demand details in writing on the letter-head of the promoter), the tax you save can be viewed as simply a reduction in costs.

As you investigate the tax concessions available, bear in mind there is generally a price to pay to enjoy these benefits. From a simple legislative barrier to spending your money before the normal retirement age to the premium price you may be asked to pay for many tax-based investments, there are costs to be taken into account as you make your decision. These are simply elements to be considered as you identify all *COSTS, BENEFITS and RISKS*. You will need to dedicate some time to investigating your options, this being one of the changes I predicted you would have to make to achieve your financial freedom.

the rich know that it's possible to change. Learn this trick too!

The rich know that it's possible to change. Learn this trick too!

Changed attitudes and changed actions

Let me assure you that it is possible to change, no matter how young or old you are. My dad said something to me recently that indicated a considerable change in his own thinking. My mum and dad (aged 70 and 80 respectively) enjoy a reasonably comfortable life, but for years I felt my dad believed he should have enjoyed a much more lucrative retirement. He is one of life's intellectuals in many ways: a compulsive reader, a long-term student of history, but also a long-term student of selling and sales management, where he made his living all of his working life. I felt for the longest time that my dad believed that his intellect should have been far more greatly rewarded. However, since he has been the sounding board for this book and for many of my public lectures and seminars over the years, his own knowledge of money and wealth creation has grown. What he said to me was: 'I had no right to expect wealth on my retirement, after all what had I ever done to create wealth?'

If you do nothing about creating wealth, then it is most likely you will create none! Most people I know – and this was true of my dad all his working life – spend 100% of their working effort on creating income. While this practice will maximise *income*, you now know that wealth and income are not the same thing. Spending all your time earning money and none of that time learning how to *keep* money will not result in anything but a life-long need to work simply to pay the bills or a retirement that promises a far inferior lifestyle than the one our income-earning years allowed us to enjoy. I must say that neither of these futures appeals to me, and if you share my view, then you need to create some time in your daily working schedule to concentrate on building your financial freedom. That is what the rich do: they not only pay attention to generating income, but they set aside time to create real wealth too – a very different activity.

if you do nothing about creating wealth, then it is most likely you will create none

You have seen that, to create the very best future possible from your financial circumstances requires new habits and new actions with your money. Avoiding taxation simply increases the amounts of money you have available for investment and the amounts of money you accumulate over your working life. Tax concessions are not only for the rich, although it is true to say that often such concessions are used only by the rich. The reason for this is that the rich approach taxation very differently from the rest of us, making their advisers aware of their desire to save tax and so ensuring they hear of all legitimate ways to reduce this cost. You, too, can act like a rich person – all you need do is seek out the right advice and act when the timing, and the investment on offer, suit you.

> you now know that wealth and income are not the same thing

Chapter 9

The rich checklist: put it into practice

The first eight chapters of this book have been dedicated to giving you the information you need to manage, invest and protect your money effectively.

The rich deal with their money in a very different manner from the rest of us and I hope that I have impressed upon you the need to change the way you think about and, perhaps even more importantly, act with money if you are going to succeed in your bid for financial freedom. Indeed, this issue is so fundamental that I believe the most important changes you need to make bear repeating.

The checklist

Take a few moments to review the summary list below:

- **Recognise financial advisers for what they are**. There is no such thing as free professional advice! Those who tell you they are financial advisers but do not charge you a fee are not financial advisers, they are product-sellers. They are people paid on commission to flog you stuff. From time to time, in order to become truly financially free, you will require the assistance

there is no such thing as free professional advice!

of an impartial financial adviser; hire one and pay him a fee. In my experience, a fee-based adviser can deliver value that far outweighs the costs of his services.

- **Stop borrowing for consumer goods**. The real 'killers' in this category are cars and many of you reading this will be paying out a fair chunk of your income each month on a car loan. Remember, every £1,000 you pay out in car repayments costs you about £2,000 in pre-tax income and could be better spent repaying a mortgage of about £163,000 over 20 years (based on a home loan interest rate of 4%).

a fee-based adviser can deliver value that far outweighs the costs of his services

  Although cars are the main culprit, many of you will have borrowed also for furniture, home entertainment systems and holidays. Change the way you do things: repay existing consumer debt as fast as you can and *never* borrow for such items again. Do as your parents, my parents, did – save for the consumer items you want and buy them with cash. Not only will you appreciate them much more, but they will also be a lot cheaper.

- **Get rid of credit cards**. As with consumer debt, the easy availability of credit is all part of making the rich that much richer and keeping the rest of us that much poorer. Do not fall for it. Do not imagine that you can have the trappings of wealth (the cars, the watches, the clothes, the holidays, etc) before you are wealthy. While it is physically possible to possess the items, possessing them is actually blocking your route to complete financial freedom. Repay those outstanding balances as fast as you can and get yourself a charge card. These offer all the convenience of a cashless

do not imagine that you can have the trappings of wealth before you are wealthy transaction but require you to pay off the balance each and every month, thus preventing you from falling into debt.

- **Pay attention to *how* you repay debt**. All debt is not bad – indeed, some debt should be repaid over as long a period as possible. Commercial debt, where the interest payments to the bank are fully tax-deductible, should generally be arranged (or renegotiated, if you already have such debt) certainly up to the limits of your retirement allowances. As retirement contributions are also fully tax-deductible, arranging commercial debt in this manner effectively means you can repay the bulk of the debt with tax-free money.
- **Consider everything before making a tax-based investment**. Far too often, the sellers of such schemes (which include property, equity and capital allowance products) concentrate on the tax-break and people rush to buy. Losing money is even less pleasant than paying tax and often, in such schemes, the investor would have been better off paying the tax and putting the net amount on deposit. Remember, these are investments first and must be acceptable to you as investments before you take the tax benefits into account. The general rule of thumb should be, if you would not invest without the tax-break, you should not invest at all! Finally, never make a tax-based investment until you have used all your available retirement allowances; they are the safest, most predictable, tax savings you can make!

if you would not invest without the tax-break, you should not invest at all!

- **Turn liabilities into assets**. Resolve today to stop thinking of your home as contributing to your wealth – the only people who will benefit from its value are your heirs. Your home produces nothing, but consumes large amounts of your income and is, therefore (as far as financial freedom is concerned),

> becoming financially free is only achievable if, once you create a little wealth, you leverage off the existing assets to create more

a liability, not an asset. This is true until you start to treat it differently, either resolving to sell it at a later date in order to downsize or using the equity you have in it to raise additional finance for investment in other assets. Becoming financially free is only achievable if, once you create a little wealth, you leverage off the existing assets to create more.

- **Change the way you earn your income**. If you are a self-employed person, earning your income as a sole trader, resolve immediately to change to a private limited company structure. Yes, this will increase slightly the costs you incur each year to comply with Revenue rules and company law – however, the benefits far outweigh those costs.

  If you are an employed person, at least have a conversation with your employer as to whether a private limited company structure would be acceptable. Do not forget there are benefits here for the employer, as they can make substantial savings too.

- **Ignore retirement allowances at your peril**. Many pension plans for sale offer bad value for money and limited scope for real investment returns. However, there are a number of vehicles, collectively known as either self-administered or self-directed pensions, that offer superb value for money and the investment flexibility, including the ability to borrow within the fund, that will lead to the opportunity of substantial real returns.

  Remember, investing in these structures allows you to keep more of the money you earn, immediately making you wealthier, and keeps your investment returns free from both income and capital gains tax. In short, the same money, invested in the same assets, achieving the same rates of return, will grow more income-producing assets inside a retirement vehicle.

- **Always remember (and use) the Golden Rules**. Becoming financially free rarely, if ever, happens by accident: you must work at it. Using the two Golden Rules will make your journey to financial freedom that bit easier. The rules are:

> becoming financially free rarely, if ever, happens by accident: you must work at it

  - Rule 1: Make money with other people's money.
  - Rule 2: Make your investments before you pay tax.

  Where Rule 1 is concerned, the simple fact is that, as long as you are getting a return on the investment that is greater than the cost of borrowing, you are making money with the bank's money.

  Properly using Rule 2 means that you keep more of the money you earn (and, where retirement funds are concerned, more of the money you make on your investments) and becoming financially free has little to do with what you *earn* and everything to do with what you *keep*!

Now you have the top tips for becoming financially free and for becoming like the rich. Not everyone will be able to implement all tips; however, even implementing one of them will improve your financial well-being.

The plan

Armed with the tools of the rich that will make you financially free, what is your next step? Well, you have to draw up a plan. To be successful, any plan must adhere to the basic rules of planning:

- It *must* be written down. Without a written plan, all you have is a vague aspiration. Once it is written down, it is a plan and can be revisited from time to time as a reminder of why you are doing what you are doing.
- It must be achievable and it must have a deadline.

The remainder of this chapter is dedicated to helping you commit your plan to paper – a plan that is achievable, albeit with some effort on your part. This plan has five phases, each of which is described in this chapter.

Phase 1: Make sure that the money you spend today is spent as efficiently as possible

Set aside a morning or afternoon to spend with that shoe box, concertina file or overflowing kitchen drawer – wherever you keep all of your financial papers.

At the back of this book are a number of planning sheets and your first task is to list everything you have. List all of your assets and all of your debts and the annual costs of those debts on the first three sheets.

Figure 2 Completing your financial freedom planning sheet 1

Step 1: Assets

What is the current value of your home? £

What is the current (cash) value of your pension(s):

Pension 1	Insert description here	£
Pension 2	Insert description here	£
Pension 3	Insert description here	£
Pension 4	Insert description here	£

If you own any investment properties, please list them here:

Property 1	Insert address here	£
Property 2	Insert address here	£
Property 3	Insert address here	£
Property 4	Insert address here	£
Property 5	Insert address here	£
Property 6	Insert address here	£

If you own any savings plans, please list them here:

Savings 1	Insert description here	£
Savings 2	Insert description here	£
Savings 3	Insert description here	£
Savings 4	Insert description here	£
Savings 5	Insert description here	£
Savings 6	Insert description here	£

If you own any other investment assets, please list them here:

Investment 1	Insert description here	£
Investment 2	Insert description here	£
Investment 3	Insert description here	£
Investment 4	Insert description here	£
Investment 5	Insert description here	£
Investment 6	Insert description here	£

Step 2: Liabilities

What is the current outstanding balance on your homeloan? £

What is the current outstanding balance on your investment property loans?

Property 1	none	£
Property 2	none	£
Property 3	none	£
Property 4	none	£
Property 5	none	£
Property 6	none	£

What is the current outstanding balance on your other investment asset loans?

Investment 1	none	£
Investment 2	none	£
Investment 3	none	£
Investment 4	none	£
Investment 5	none	£
Investment 6	none	£

If you have any consumer debt, please enter details below.

Overdraft?	Insert description here	£
Car loans?	Insert description here	£
Credit Cards?	Insert description here	£
Store Cards?	Insert description here	£
Hire Purchase Debt?	Insert description here	£

If you have any other short-term debt, please list below.

Additional Debt 1	Insert description here	£
Additional Debt 2	Insert description here	£
Additional Debt 3	Insert description here	£
Additional Debt 4	Insert description here	£
Additional Debt 5	Insert description here	£
Additional Debt 6	Insert description here	£

Step 3: Monthly outgoings

What is the monthly cost of your home loan? £ per month

What is the monthly cost of your investment mortgages?

Property 1	none	£	per month
Property 2	none	£	per month
Property 3	none	£	per month
Property 4	none	£	per month
Property 5	none	£	per month
Property 6	none	£	per month

What is the monthly cost of your other investment assets?

Investment 1	none	£	per month
Investment 2	none	£	per month
Investment 3	none	£	per month
Investment 4	none	£	per month
Investment 5	none	£	per month
Investment 6	none	£	per month

What is the monthly cost of your pensions?

Pension 1	none	£	per month
Pension 2	none	£	per month
Pension 3	none	£	per month
Pension 4	none	£	per month

What is the monthly cost of your savings?

Savings 1	none	£	per month
Savings 2	none	£	per month
Savings 3	none	£	per month
Savings 4	none	£	per month
Savings 5	none	£	per month
Savings 6	none	£	per month

What is the monthly cost of your consumer debt?

Overdraft?	none	£	per month
Car loans?	none	£	per month
Credit Cards?	none	£	per month
Store Cards?	none	£	per month
Hire Purchase Debt?	none	£	per month

What is the monthly cost of your other short-term debt?

Additional Debt 1	none	£	per month
Additional Debt 2	none	£	per month
Additional Debt 3	none	£	per month
Additional Debt 4	none	£	per month
Additional Debt 5	none	£	per month
Additional Debt 6	none	£	per month

Once you have completed this task, you need to begin taking the new actions that are going to make you financially free. The place to start is with those **consumer debts**! *You must plan to repay these as quickly as possible.* 'Where will the money come from?', I hear you yell. This, of course, is where you start to sacrifice. It is most unlikely that any savings accounts you have, for example, are achieving returns in excess of the cost of these loans. So the first thing to do is to stop saving, cash in your chips and use the cash value to pay off the most expensive loan. If you have cash left, repay the second most expensive loan, and so on until your savings are spent. Now, use the money you were paying into the savings to accelerate the monthly repayments on the most expensive of the remaining loans. When that loan is repaid, apply the amount you had been paying to the next most expensive loan and continue to do this until all consumer debt has been repaid.

For some readers, repaying consumer debt will take months; for others, it may take years; but no matter how long it takes, it makes complete financial sense. You cannot invest money without surplus income and these debts are eating your income alive. Many readers will empathise with the situation where all of your income is committed even before you earn it and, in my experience, consumer debt is the major offender.

As you embark on the repayment of expensive debt, there are other things you can do as well. Next, you should concentrate on any **commercial loans** (typically, loans for a business or to purchase buy-to-let property) and call your lender for an appointment. At the meeting, you will tell your banker (and I mean *tell*, not ask) that you wish to change your loan(s) to a retirement-backed structure. Depending on your personal allowances, you may be able to alter all loans to this more tax-efficient repayment method, but you should be able to take some advantage at least.

One note of caution here: many of the major lenders either own, or are owned by, a life insurance company and may try to sell you the pension for the retirement-backed structure. *Do not fall for this!* The pension will be overladen with internal charges, which undermine its ability to perform. In truth, even for the most financially astute, it may be necessary to have a professional to assist you with this element of your financial restructuring. Make sure he is fee-based and agree the fee in advance.

Keep the tricks of the rich in mind: if you already have some form of retirement plan, it may be possible to use it for this restructuring. If not, then ensure your fee-based adviser can handle the retirement scheme too and will do so for a fee (quoted and agreed in advance). Once this restructuring is complete, you will be paying less income tax and, as a result, your loan(s) will be considerably cheaper to service and repay.

Phase 2: Set your financial freedom target

You are now on the road to financial freedom. You are changing the way you think about money and, all-importantly, the way you act with money. You have put some of these changes into action. It is now about time to identify where you are going. Phase 2 of your new plan is to set your target.

To identify your accurate lifestyle income, you must return to your spreadsheets and complete the final one.

Your lifestyle income is the average monthly amount you spend on light, heat, clothing, holidays, transport, etc. To calculate it, you need to take away from your income the non-lifestyle expenses (the mortgage, the car loan and other consumer debts) as well as the future savings being made (the pension contributions and other savings). The next thing to do is to inflate this figure into the future, to the date when financial freedom can be achieved. (See the future value calculator in Appendix 1 and multiply your current figure by the relevant number. Use the 4.5% per annum multiplier as that assumes that your income will rise at a slightly higher rate than the long-term inflation figure assumed throughout this volume.)

Figure 3 Completing your financial freedom planning sheet 2

Step 4: Your financial freedom target

Income Details				
Insert your After-Tax Earned Income		£		
Insert your After-Tax Rental Income		£		
TOTAL NET INCOME		£	**0**	per annum
Non-Lifestyle Expenses				
Homeloan Mortgage	£ 0 monthly =	£	0	per annum
Investment Mortgages	£ 0 monthly =	£	0	per annum
Pension Contributions	£ 0 monthly =	£	0	per annum
Savings Plans	£ 0 monthly =	£	0	per annum
Consumer Debt	£ 0 monthly =	£	0	per annum
Other Short-term Debt	£ 0 monthly =	£	0	per annum
TOTAL NON-LIFESTYLE EXPENSES		£	**0**	per annum
Annual Lifestyle Income				
Total Net Income	less Total Non-Lifestyle Expenses	£	**0**	per annum
Financial Freedom Target				
What age are you?	In how any years do you plan to achieve your Financial Freedom?			years
The future value of your Annual Lifestyle Income in	years will be...	£	**0**	per annum
The Target Fund for your Financial Freedom is....	**£0**			

Now you have your true lifestyle costs, inflated into the future, and you should turn to the ready reckoner on page 173 to find your financial freedom target. It may be difficult to decide on a period of time within which to achieve financial freedom, so my suggestion is that, at least initially, you start by planning to your 60th birthday – wouldn't financial freedom make a nice birthday present! – or, if you are already close to or over 60, use a five-year period initially.

So you can now see that your financial freedom target is £__________ (*insert your figure here*) in ____ (*insert the number of years to go here*) years' time.

Now, probably for the first time in your life, you have a specific financial target to meet in a specific timeframe – in other words, you have a plan to achieve financial freedom.

You have completed Phase 2 of your plan. You know exactly how much you need to accumulate in investment assets, over a specific timeframe, so that you can become financially free. Simply knowing this figure gives you a huge advantage over most people; it is a real number and, as high as it might seem, armed with your new-found financial knowledge, you can set about planning how you are going to get there.

You are moving into Phase 3 of your plan.

Phase 3: Calculate how far you have already travelled

Now that you have started to undo the errors of the past and are, for the first time, in possession of your financial freedom target, it is time to judge how much of the journey you have already completed.

Here, you will have to do a little work with your calculator. Set out in Appendix 1 of this book is a table that allows you to estimate the value of your existing financial freedom assets at your financial freedom target date. There are two future growth assumption columns: one that assumes those assets grow at 4.5% per annum, and the other which assumes 6% per annum. You now know that these figures are of little importance unless and until inflation is taken into account. Assuming a long-term inflation rate of 3% per annum, what these growth rates predict is that certain assets you hold will grow at a rate of 1.5% above inflation, while others will increase in value at 3% above inflation. Earlier I referred to this figure as the 'real yield', the only figure that is of importance as it expresses the growth above inflation. Do not forget that if you are getting a real yield of less than inflation, you are losing money, not making it, no matter whether the bottom-line value is increasing or not. If you have forgotten this message, please reread the section on risk in Chapter 4.

These are standard future value assumptions that we use in our business, where we use the real yield of 1.5% per annum above inflation to estimate the value of guaranteed investments, such as long-term (3 years+) deposit accounts and government loan stock (gilts/bonds). Typically, we use the 3% per annum real yield assumption for property or equity (stocks and shares) assets.

So, let us assume that you have a long-term cash deposit of £10,000 at present and that your financial planning period is 14 years. What will your deposit be worth in 14 years' time? Table 4 tells us. You can see that the table tells us to multiply your £10,000 by 1.85, giving an estimated future value of £18,500.

Table 4 Extract from future value calculator*

Years to financial freedom	Multiplier for growth of 4.5% *per annum*	Multiplier for growth of 6% *per annum*
14	1.85	2.26

* The full calculator is shown in Appendix 1.

Now let us assume that you have an investment property valued at £200,000. What will it be worth in 14 years' time? This time the calculator tells us to use the multiple of 2.26, which gives us an estimated value of £452,000 in 14 years.

Continue down your list of assets, applying the appropriate multiple, and write down these values on a separate sheet. If you have regular savings plans, such as pensions, for example, you will need to write to the company or your adviser – or was he a 'seller' rather than an adviser? – and get estimated values at your financial freedom date. Once you get these, input them on your separate sheet. You should now be able to total your future value and compare this to the financial freedom target you calculated in Phase 20.

Any shortfall in your current planning is now obvious, as that shortfall is the difference between the figures you have just calculated and your financial freedom target.

Assuming you have identified a shortfall (most people do!), please fill it in the space below.

Shortfall: £________

Having identified this shortfall, the first thing you can do is to investigate the possibility of raising further finance on your home: you should be able to raise the mortgage to at least 70% of the value of the house. Get out your calculator and calculate 70% of the value you have placed on your house and take from this figure the existing mortgage amount; now you have the amount of equity release a lender should offer. This figure becomes your 30% deposit on new property purchase.

Example 7

Equity release from your home

Value of home	£300,000
70% of home value	£210,000
Current mortgage	£100,000
Equity release potential	£110,000
New property purchase price	£366,650*

*This is the amount that you could spend on new property investments (including all costs and fees)

I am not for a moment suggesting that getting this type of financial support from a bank is easy, especially now, as the credit crunch bites deepest. What I am drawing your attention to is the potential for the maximisation of your own financial future by using *all* of your assets to create sustainable financial security. That is one of the greatest tricks of the rich and is often what sets them apart from the rest. Some of the risks may be too high, but please remember there is also a substantial risk in doing nothing. If you cannot bring yourself to apply the tricks of the rich, then what type of financial future awaits? Without independently building your own financial security, you will be dependent on the state, and that is a future few relish.

some of the risks may be too high, but there is also a substantial risk in doing nothing

Back to our example: always assuming a lender will grant you the 70% loan-to-value (LTV) debt, you could spend an additional £366,650 on investment properties. It is time to go and visit your lender, *not yet time to try to find a suitable property!*

Phase 3 of your plan is now all but complete. The only other matter you need consider is what to do with any surplus income your planning and restructuring has identified. Once again, I have no hesitation in recommending that any surplus should be put to work inside your retirement plan – at least until you have reached your maximum allowances. There is no better way of saving tax and, as long as the charges are not too prohibitive, no better way of building wealth. As suggested earlier, it is time to seek out some professional help and get yourself a private pension fund.

What to do now

Some of you may have even greater surpluses than can be taken care of by retirement allowances. Congratulations first of all – your restructuring has obviously been very successful! Second, you will need other things to do with your money and, hopefully, the previous chapters will have suggested some projects. If you need more help, here are a few tips.

Get yourself on as many mailing lists as you can

There are many, many money-making and tax-saving projects available to the private investor at any given time. Some will be the more ordinary, off-the-shelf, financial products, where you have to be very careful about the charges levied. Others will be more exclusive, and usually better-value, projects, generally promoted by one, or a small number, of the more innovative financial advisory firms.

You need to be aware of as many opportunities as possible, so let people know you are in the market. Contact a number of auctioneers and, having negotiated your finance deal, tell them the type of investment property you are after. Get in touch with some accountancy firms and tell them you are interested in tax-breaks. Call the fee-based financial advisers and tell them of your interests. These firms, which are always keen to win new clients, should have no problem in placing you on their marketing lists, thus substantially improving the number of investment and tax-saving opportunities that come your way.

Read everything you can about money, becoming rich, successful investing, etc

Knowledge is power and the more knowledge you possess, the more powerful, in financial terms at least, you will become.

Nobody is born knowing how to manage money; after all, money is not natural and so our instinct can do nothing for us. Not only this but also, for the most part, formal education teaches us little or nothing about money either. I had a meeting recently with a client who is a prosthodontist, a qualification for which he went through 22 years of formal education. He told me that, in those 22 years, he never received even one class about money and how to manage it – and he believed that was deliberate.

the more knowledge you possess, the more powerful, in financial terms at least, you will become

He is not alone. There is a school of thought which suggests that, based on the history of formal education, it is deliberate that most of us are taught very little about money. The modern education system, it seems, has its roots in the Industrial Revolution, when the schools were established with the help of the industrialists. These men were keen to have a more educated workforce, yet were not, it is said, keen to have their employees educated too much – otherwise they would be creating competition for themselves. Thus, the curriculum that was taught, and which, with just a few modern additions, is the curriculum that is still taught, did not teach the employees about money.

While my own knowledge of the history of formal education does not allow me to make a definitive conclusion, this version of its history has more than a ring of truth to me. Back then, just as it remains today, the vast majority of the world's wealth was controlled by a tiny minority of the population and then, like now, the rich would like to keep it that way.

Whether this interpretation is true or not, the unarguable fact is that most of us, no matter how many years we spend in formal education, leave school knowing little or nothing about money. This means that it is up to us to educate ourselves and this is why I recommend you read everything you can about the subject.

Feel the fear, but do it anyway

The journey to financial freedom is not easy and one of the hardest things you will have to deal with is the voice inside your head which tells you that you cannot do this or that. We all experience it – it causes that feeling in the pit of your stomach, as if an invisible hand had reached in, grabbed your guts, and twisted them a half-turn. This is fear and it has the potential to paralyse us completely.

The first thing I want to assure you is that everyone feels fear – and I mean everyone! So the fact that you feel the fear is neither a flaw in your personality nor is it a barrier to you reaching financial freedom. It is how you deal with the fear that will dictate whether you actually achieve your dreams.

it is how you deal with the fear that will dictate whether you actually achieve your dreams

My father's father was a medic at the Battle of the Somme, one of history's most infamous battles, where far too many young men lost their lives due to the inadequacies of a small number of old men. You can imagine the fear that my grandfather and the rest of his comrades felt as they waited for the order to go over the top. However, it was the way these men dealt with the fear that made them heroes or cowards, not feeling the fear itself, since the fear was, according to my grandfather, universal.

I read a story recently about two men awaiting the order to go over the top; both had knotted insides; both shuffled from foot to foot, knuckles whitened as they held their rifles tightly. Both men thought of their loved ones back home and each fought back a tear as they admitted to themselves that they might never see them again. Both, quite frankly, were scared out of their minds, and who could blame them?

The order was given and both were helped over the top by the throng of soldiers waiting behind them, bullets immediately whizzing about their heads. One man stayed in control, charged an enemy machine gun and singlehandedly took the enemy position. The other man lost control and collapsed to the ground, tears flowing uncontrollably, paralysed and unable to move.

The first man was a hero and won a medal for his bravery, the second was branded a coward. Both men felt exactly the same emotion. Both were understandably scared. They just dealt with that emotion differently.

And here is the point: everyone feels fear where their money is concerned. You will feel it and it is completely understandable. How you deal with it will dictate your financial future.

Diversify and learn by your mistakes

Different types of investment assets perform at different stages of the economic cycle. Diversifying your investments should mean that, no matter what stage of the economic cycle, some of your investments are doing well.

Everyone knows the saying: 'Don't put all your eggs in one basket'. It's just as relevant in the financial business as it is in any other. Learn about all of the different investment assets – property, stocks and shares, bonds and cash deposits – and invest across the range.

Also, do not expect that every investment you make will be successful. As in all walks of life, you will fail sometimes – although a diversified portfolio of investments means that any failure will have a limited impact on your overall wealth. Failure is not to be feared or frowned upon; it is, in fact, the greatest teacher of all.

There is a saying: 'Success is no teacher', which is absolutely true. Indeed, it is a human trait that we learn by making mistakes. The problem with money is that making a mistake and losing a few bob tends to mean most people give up. Imagine if you had applied this logic to everything you have learned so far. Imagine if, when learning to ride a bike, you had given up when you had your first fall. You would never have learned to ride a bike. The same is true as you learn to become financially free; if you give up at your first mistake, then you will never get there.

> failure is not to be feared or frowned upon; it is the greatest teacher of all

You will make mistakes but, as with the fear discussed in the previous section, it is how you deal with the mistakes that will dictate the final outcome. Also, it is the damage to your overall plan that your errors cause that will impact on your planning process and this is why the broad spread of different investments is suggested. Of course, not everyone will be able to diversify immediately. You simply may not have enough capital to spread around. Do not let this fact stop you from starting your plan, but do pay attention as you progress that plan in the future.

Finally, remember this, if nothing else: the only person who never makes a mistake is the person who never tries!

Phase 4: What happens if 'the wheels fall off'?

You have made a great start; your plan is in place; you know what your financial freedom target is and you know when it can be achieved. In addition, you have identified the major financial errors of the past and have started to put them right. For the first time in your financial life, you have started to take control and you deserve hearty congratulations for your efforts. Very few people have your financial ambitions and even fewer actually do anything about those ambitions.

You have already seen that an important part of financial planning is identifying the risks being taken. Phase 4 of your plan is about dealing with two of the greatest of these:

- What happens if you die?
- What happens if you get so ill that you cannot work?

Death and long-term disability are the two greatest risks to your long-term financial plan. Income is the lifeblood of financial planning and, without ongoing income, your plan will fail.

Death

If you plan to reach financial freedom, my view is that you should plan to reach it no matter what happens.

income is the lifeblood of financial planning and, without ongoing income, your plan will fail

For those of you who are unattached, without dependants, the need for death insurance is limited. I believe that the only death cover needed in these circumstances is enough to cover your debts. No matter who might inherit your estate if you were to die prematurely, inheriting debt-free will mean a very easy inheritance. Inheriting assets that still have outstanding debts attaching will require a considerable amount of work, time and expense for the beneficiary. The real problem here is the expenses – it is not uncommon for many unstructured estates to give more value to the lawyers and financial advisers than to the actual beneficiary.

Death insurance to cover loans is relatively inexpensive, although it does pay to shop around. Do not simply accept the quote you are given by the lender. Take that quote to an impartial adviser and see what they can do for you. In most cases, the impartial adviser should be able to lessen the costs, improve the benefits or both.

If you have dependants – a spouse and/or children – you also need to cover all of your debts with death insurance and should follow the advice above. However, you have additional cover to implement.

As I travelled my own route to financial freedom, I wanted to ensure that, if I died before I got there, my wife and family were fast-tracked to financial freedom. If you think about it, Phase 2 of my plan told me what my financial freedom target was, while Phase 3 illustrated for me how far I had already travelled. The death insurance I needed was the gap between the two figures. Not only was the amount of cover needed quite obvious, but I only needed that cover until I reached financial freedom and, in any event, as the years passed by, my need for cover would reduce. As my assets increased in value, the gap between where I was and where I wanted to be would narrow, and so, the wealthier I became, the less death insurance I would need.

So why then did I have whole-of-life insurance that was escalating each year in line with inflation? The answer, of course, is that was what the insurance companies had told me I needed – not surprisingly, the 'advice' suited them more than me. Death insurance, (which is sold under the name of 'life insurance', as very few would buy it at all if it used its proper name) is mostly sold to us rather than being sought out. Commission (the way insurance salespeople are remunerated) is a percentage of the cost of such insurance; therefore, the higher the cost, the higher the income to the seller. As whole-of-life cover is significantly more expensive than the limited-term version, the income for the salesperson is considerably more.

Having performed the financial calculations of Phases 2 and 3, you know what death insurance you need. It is simply the gap between the financial freedom target and your current net asset value (NAV). While it could be argued that the amount of cover needed is actually somewhat less (since the financial freedom target is a future value and the NAV figure is a current value), it is too complex and beyond the scope of this book to outline how you might calculate annualised inflation discounts. If you use the figure I have suggested you will definitely have adequate cover, and perhaps a little extra that, let's face it, would not go amiss if the family had just lost a parent and major breadwinner. If, God forbid, you were to die prematurely, your family would receive a major cash payment, immediately making them financially free. They will have problems, of course, after losing their spouse, mother or father, but they will not have financial problems.

Please fill in below the amount of death insurance that you have calculated you need:

Death insurance £ ____________

and how long until financial freedom:

____ **years to financial freedom**

This is the amount of life insurance you need and you only need it for the period of years shown.

You can now seek quotations for death cover for this figure over your planning term, making sure that you ask for a 'convertible term' policy. The 'convertible' element ensures that cover can be extended, without additional medical evidence having to be produced, if for some reason you fail to reach your financial freedom target in the original timeframe.

If you are lucky enough to have death benefit paid for you by your employer, via the company's superannuation (pension) fund, then keep it – why not, if it is paid for by someone else!

Having calculated the cover required, you may find that you have it already; many of my clients actually have too much cover. No matter what cover is in place, you should now seek quotes, from an impartial agent, for replacement cover on a fixed-term convertible policy. Once you know the price of the new cover, you can decide whether to keep your existing cover or replace it.

Disability

Here I am referring to long-term disability, the kind that can leave you without any ability, or a much-curtailed ability, to earn money in the future. Many readers will have some existing protection in this area, again via your employer's superannuation scheme. However, such cover is usually quite limited.

I am of the opinion that, in the event of long-term disability, your income should not be affected at all. Most disability benefit schemes (known as 'permanent health insurance') only provide a maximum benefit of two-thirds income, less the state disability benefits to which you are entitled. What this means is that, in the event that you suffer a long-term disability, your income is guaranteed to reduce by at least one-third. I say 'at least', because such cover generally only applies to basic salary, so any bonus or overtime income is not covered at all.

The only way that you can ensure your complete income is covered is to use a combination of two types of policy: the first being the permanent health insurance (PHI) mentioned already; the second being critical illness cover. PHI pays out an income, while critical illness policies pay out a lump sum.

If you already have some PHI benefits, subtract this figure from your gross income. You have now identified the amount of pre-tax income you would lose in the event of a long-term disability. (If you do not have any PHI benefits, then your total income needs to be covered in some other way.) This shortfall figure needs to be grossed up to an amount that (if you need to make a claim), once invested in a relatively risk-free environment, will replace lost income between the date of disability and your financial freedom target date.

Again, you need to get out the calculator here to calculate the amount of critical illness cover you need – Example 8 shows how you might do this for yourself; one set of calculations illustrates the lower income tax rate, the other the higher rate. All you need do is apply the same maths to your own figures and then you can set about buying the cover.

Note that this method of calculating the cover required is not ideal, as it takes no account of inflation into the future, which will erode your capital. However, without getting into truly complex financial calculations that are beyond the scope of this book, it will give you an excellent level of cover and will protect your income long-term, which is its purpose. For example, if we assume a 3% per annum erosion of capital due to inflation, the lump sums calculated in Example 8 would last for 33+ years, probably well beyond your financial freedom date.

Example 8

Calculating critical illness cover

Gross (pre-tax) annual income:	£26,000
Existing PHI benefits, paying annual income of:	£10,000
Loss in gross income after claim:	£16,000
Tax (@ 20%) on lost income:	£3,200
Shortfall in net (after-tax) income:	£12,800
Long-term growth assumption:	4.5% per annum
Critical illness requirement:	**£284,445**

(calculated as £12,800 ÷ 4.5 × 100 = £284,445)

Gross (pre-tax) annual income:	£100,000
Existing PHI benefits, paying annual income of:	£60,000
Loss in gross income after claim:	£40,000
Tax (@ 40%) on lost income:	£16,000
Shortfall in net (after-tax) income:	£24,000
Long-term guaranteed growth assumption:	4.5% per annum
Critical illness requirement:	**£533,333**
(calculated as £24,000 ÷ 4.5 × 100 = £533,333)	

If you do not have any PHI benefits, then the first thing to do (after you get details of your state benefits) is find out how much of your income can be covered by a personal PHI policy (talk to an independent agent) and, once you know that amount, follow Example 8 to calculate the amount of critical illness cover you require.

A few words of caution here. Firstly, you must realise that PHI benefits are very different from those provided by critical illness cover.

PHI pays a taxable income in the event of a successful claim and may pay that income, rising each year, up to a predetermined 'retirement' date (payments are reviewed regularly to ensure claimants are not abusing the system). A successful claim is any medically provable event that keeps you from working, with the claim being paid until either you return to work or you reach your 'retirement' date. (Proportionate claims can be made if you are able to return to a job that pays less than your pre-illness empolyment.) Thus, a PHI policy may pay a short-term claim – for example, if you broke both legs and your work requires you to drive – or a long-term claim in the event that your illness or injury keeps you from ever working again.

A critical illness policy, on the other hand, pays a one-off claim, as a tax-free lump sum, should you suffer one of the major illnesses as defined in the policy conditions. Therefore, it is not a policy designed to assist you in the 'broken legs' scenario, but only comes into play if you have suffered one of the 'nasty' illnesses (heart attack, cancer, stroke, etc). Your finances should be such that your financial freedom plan could survive a short-term drop in income (PHI generally has a 'deferred period', during which no income is payable), even if it could not survive a long-term drop. In the event that you are unfortunate enough to suffer long-term disability, you are more than likely to have suffered one of the 'nasties' and thus the critical illness plan should pay out exactly when you need it.

Once you have calculated the level of cover you need, look for a quotation. Make sure you choose an impartial financial adviser who has access to all of the product-providers, since this reduces the effort you need to make to get the best price.

Proper insurance cover is not cheap but, in my view, it is absolutely vital as you make your new financial plan. It is certainly one of the tricks of the rich to have enough (but never too much or too expensive) money made available to heirs after death, so that the other assets they built up are unencumbered (without debt attaching) and freely available to those they leave behind. None of these policies will pay out if you do not claim during the term (they will not have any investment element or any potential encashment value), and so could be viewed, especially in hindsight, as a waste of money. However, let me assure you, no widow or widower has ever complained about a waste of money as they receive their spouse's life insurance cheque. I believe that your plan for financial freedom should not be dependent upon 'luck'. Certainly, I would never promise my wife and family that we will be financially free as long as I do not die or do not get sick – that is no promise at all.

It is true that the right death and disability cover is expensive and probably will cost more money than you are used to paying for such cover. But remember, from the very start of this book, I challenged you to think differently about money, while also counselling you that, if you are not prepared to change your views, you cannot achieve financial freedom. Ensuring that, no matter what personal disaster strikes, including premature death or long-term disability, you achieve financial freedom for yourself or your family is one of those changes you have to make. The death notices in today's papers are filled with the names of people who did not believe they would die yesterday. Our hospitals' accident and emergency rooms today are filled with people who did not believe they would be sick yesterday. The greatest risk to your and your family's financial future is your health. If, heaven forbid, you are struck down, do not let your financial dreams die (or let your family lose theirs) at the same time.

Phase 5: Review regularly

If there is one prediction one can make confidently about the future, it is that it will be different from today. Change is inevitable and marches on whether we like it or not. As it does so, your financial plan may need to change too.

your financial plan may need to change

Your own circumstances will alter: you may be promoted, change jobs, get married, get divorced, have a child (or more children), inherit money, win the lottery, etc. Any one of these changes in your circumstances will mean some knock-on changes to your plans: some will be positive, others negative, but, no matter which, you will have to react.

Outside your personal world, other changes may affect your plans: interest rate rises, currency revaluations, stock market fluctuations, the general economic climate, tax rates, legislative alterations, etc. Again, any one of these has the potential to change your overall plans – and you either react to such changes or you abandon your plan.

Planning your financial freedom is not only about putting things right today, but also ensuring that they remain right throughout the rest of your financial life. The way you used to deal with your money is most comfortable for you (it is only human nature to be attracted to the things we know best) and, unless you are diligent, you could lapse back into the old patterns.

For all of these reasons, it is imperative that you review your plan on a regular basis. At least once a year, sit down with your planning sheets or spreadsheet and fill in the new numbers, which will give you new targets. Each year, review your financial life, always asking whether you are getting the very best value for money.

review your plan on a regular basis

Always ensure that your product-providers (banks, building societies, insurance companies, fund managers, etc) give you an annual report on the business you have with them and tell them when you want it. Get all of these reports at the same time of the year and sit down and review your plans.

Remember, pay attention to the two Golden Rules: simply applying them where you can will mean that you will become better off than you ever imagined possible.

Chapter 10

Do it – or stop moaning about money!

I have been a prolific reader of this type of book for much of my working life and they have all had one common problem: for any book of this nature to truly help any reader, *the reader must take action!*

I read statistics on this particular matter recently. Only one in 10 readers will do anything at all with the lessons they learn from such a publication and only one in 100 readers will make permanent changes and achieve their financial goals. Your purchase of this book will make me a little wealthier but buying it and reading it will not, in themselves, do anything for you.

The fact that you are reading the book at all means you are curious about financial freedom and how it might be achieved, but that is all it means. I hope that *Tricks of the Rich* has shown you that building assets to replace your income (without the necessity to work) is possible for everyone, whether they earn lots of money or a little. I hope that it has shown you that you and your family can be financially free.

> true financial freedom is won at a price – the price being your own effort

What it has not shown you is that achieving financial freedom is easy, because it is not easy! What it has shown you is that true financial freedom is won at a price – the price being your own effort, first, to truly understand the methods you can use to improve your financial well-being and, second, to take action.

Motivation

I recently attended a training course on managing a business, which concentrated heavily on how one might manage and motivate people. The presenter told us that a common error made by 'people managers' is that they attempt to manage the actions of their people. He told us that, before you can manage actions, you have to identify what drives those people to those actions.

He drew the following simple diagram:

Desire leads to ➔ **Actions** lead to ➔ **Results**

As soon as he put this up on his flipchart, it seemed perfectly logical and I questioned why I had never thought of it before. Of course, people are driven to action by their desires – it is so blindingly obvious.

The point I am trying to make is that you need to really desire financial freedom, if you are going to take the actions necessary to achieve the required results. I have never spoken to anyone about financial freedom and had them tell me it is a bad idea. Everyone would like to achieve financial freedom. Everyone would like to be able to choose to work if they wanted, not because they have to. However, not everyone wants it enough to make the changes they need to make in how they think and act with regard to their money.

> you need to really desire financial freedom, if you are going to take the actions necessary to achieve the required results

Be sure that you are not one of those people. You have already taken the first step and, as the old Chinese proverb says, 'Even the longest journey starts with just one step.' You have started the journey and, by reading this book, you have given yourself the tools required to take the next step and the one after that. You go into this process with your eyes wide open. You know it is not going to be easy.

Effort and resolve

There will be fear along the way, the fear that taking risks instils in all of us, no matter who we are. However, the fear will not be a surprise; you are ready for it and prepared to 'feel the fear and do it anyway'. There will also be pain along the journey. You will deny yourself those consumer goods that you used to buy with expensive debt. Your car may not be as 'cool' as it once was; your holidays may be taken that little bit closer to home; and you may redecorate your house less often than you would previously. However, as you feel this pain, remind yourself that it has been these expensive consumer debts that have stood in the way of your fantastic financial future. Remind yourself that those who buy consumer goods in this manner are making the world's richest people richer and themselves poorer. When your neighbour has a 'cooler' car than you, you now know it does not necessarily mean he is richer than you. It probably means he has not learned the lessons that you have learned. If someone you know has a bigger home, that is no indication of wealth. You now know that the home is not an asset, it is a liability and the person with the bigger home has greater liabilities than you. Such people are, in my opinion, more to be pitied than envied. They will come to the realisation some day, just as my own parents did, that the family home does nothing for the wealth of the current generation and only makes the next generation richer.

> if you decide to change nothing, you should also abandon your dream of financial freedom

All of this being said, having read and understood this book, you may decide that you do not have the desire. If you are not willing to make the sacrifices needed, not willing to tolerate the pain and fear that come hand-in-hand with striving towards financial freedom, then that is a legitimate decision too. You have reached your decision from a fully informed position and you are to be applauded for the courage that that decision takes. However, remember, if you decide to change nothing, you should also abandon your dream of financial freedom, because it is only a pipe-dream.

Of course, there will always be exceptions to any rule. We can always find someone who, through luck, marriage, or simply by being in the right place at the right time, became financially free without any sacrifice. Do not kid yourself, such people are very much the exception, not the rule. The vast majority of people who reach financial freedom do so because they have made sacrifices; they have taken risks and worked hard to educate themselves about the ways in which the financial world works. The odds of you achieving financial freedom are exponentially increased if you make a plan, exercise proper financial controls, use proper financial structures and work damn hard.

Advice

This book has been written to give you the basic knowledge needed to understand the tricks of the rich and to plan your financial freedom. It does, as I am sure you have already realised, take dedication of time and effort on your part. However, as a financial adviser who specialises in managing the financial freedom journey for my clients, it would be remiss of me not to suggest that you do not, of course, have to do it yourself.

While using a professional adviser adds a layer of cost, it is better to pay those costs than simply never find the time. Better to pay someone like me to do the job for you than not to have the job done. Fees are not necessarily a bad thing. As my grandfather used to say: 'Never worry about what the other fellow is earning if you are happy with what you are earning yourself.' If you actually achieve financial freedom, when you can have your lifestyle without ever working again, surely that is worth paying for?

Also, remember that, while I have given you the basics in this book, a true professional adviser will know not just these but will have some other tricks up his sleeve. They are working in this area all of the time and encounter new ideas and new products daily. You will grow in knowledge and experience as you develop your plan but it is unlikely that you will ever have the time that the professional has available.

> you will grow in knowledge and experience but it is unlikely that you will ever have the time that the professional has available

If you are avoiding fees because you are just not used to paying them and find them hard to swallow, *stop*! You are still thinking the way you used to before this book challenged you to think differently. Remember, this type of thinking has brought you to your current financial position and you are unlikely to be reading this if you are blissfully happy with that position. If you are avoiding the fee simply to save a few pounds, don't do that!

I recently attended the 40th birthday celebrations of a friend who sells lawn mowers for a living. In giving his brief speech to thank us all for attending and his wife for her Trojan work, he could not resist one lawn mower pitch. The machines he imports and distributes are well known and relatively expensive, so he repeated his now famous sales line:

'If you buy cheap, you buy twice.'

As soon as the words were out of his mouth, I knew I had to get them into this book – they are just so powerful and so true. Do not avoid the fees of a truly impartial adviser because you want to buy cheap. It is a false economy. Neither should you throw fees at anyone who claims to be able to help you achieve your goals. You need to meet with them; convince yourself they really know what they are doing; ask them to outline some of their past successes; get an introduction to an existing client; ask the difficult questions. You are now armed with more good financial ideas than most so-called financial 'advisers' will ever have and thus you will be better able to sort the advisers from the product-sellers.

If cash and/or cash flow is stopping you from paying a professional, then there is no doubt that you can use the tricks of this book to manage your own journey to financial freedom. You will need a little more determination and dedication to achieve your goals, but they will taste all the sweeter when you do reach them.

the first thing you have to change is your mind

Remember, the first thing you have to change, if you are to learn the tricks of the rich and to become financially free, is your *mind.*

Appendix 1

Future value calculator

Years to financial freedom	Multiplier for growth of 4.5% p.a.	Multiplier for growth of 6% p.a.
1	1.045	1.060
2	1.092	1.124
3	1.141	1.191
4	1.193	1.263
5	1.246	1.338
6	1.302	1.419
7	1.361	1.504
8	1.422	1.594
9	1.486	1.690
10	1.553	1.791
11	1.623	1.898
12	1.696	2.012
13	1.772	2.133
14	1.852	2.261
15	1.935	2.396
16	2.022	2.540
17	2.113	2.693
18	2.209	2.854
19	2.308	3.026
20	2.412	3.207
21	2.520	3.399
22	2.633	3.604
23	2.752	3.820
24	2.876	4.049
25	3.005	4.292
26	3.141	4.549
27	3.282	4.822
28	3.429	5.111
29	3.584	5.418
30	3.745	5.744
31	3.914	6.088

Years to financial freedom	Multiplier for growth of 4.5% p.a.	Multiplier for growth of 6% p.a.
32	4.090	6.453
33	4.274	6.841
34	4.466	7.251
35	4.667	7.686
36	4.877	8.147
37	5.097	8.636
38	5.326	9.154
39	5.566	9.704
40	5.816	10.286

Appendix 2

Financial freedom planning sheets

Financial Freedom Calculator

About the Financial Freedom Calculator

This calculator is designed to help you to calculate the capital sum you will need at your ***Financial Freedom Target Date*** in order to replace your ***Lifestyle Income***. Simply enter as much relevant information on the Assets, Liabilities, and Monthly Outgoing tables that follow. Follow the instructions outlined in Chapter 9 to complete the subsequent tables and you will arrive at your own ***Financial Freedom Target***.

Some Terms

Lifestyle Income: the amount of money that you spend on yourself, after you pay your other monthly financial commitments (mortgages, pensions, credit cards, etc.)

Financial Freedom: the ability to replace your lifestyle income without having to continue working.

Financial Freedom Target: the minimum capital sum that you will require in order to replace your lifestyle income.

Assets

What is the current value of your home?		£	
What is the current (cash) value of your pension(s):			
Pension 1	Insert description here	£	
Pension 2	Insert description here	£	
Pension 3	Insert description here	£	
Pension 4	Insert description here	£	
If you own any investment properties, please list them here:			
Property 1	Insert address here	£	
Property 2	Insert address here	£	
Property 3	Insert address here	£	
Property 4	Insert address here	£	
Property 5	Insert address here	£	
Property 6	Insert address here	£	
If you own any savings plans, please list them here:			
Savings 1	Insert description here	£	
Savings 2	Insert description here	£	
Savings 3	Insert description here	£	
Savings 4	Insert description here	£	
Savings 5	Insert description here	£	
Savings 6	Insert description here	£	
If you own any other investment assets, please list them here:			
Investment 1	Insert description here	£	
Investment 2	Insert description here	£	
Investment 3	Insert description here	£	
Investment 4	Insert description here	£	
Investment 5	Insert description here	£	
Investment 6	Insert description here	£	

Liabilities

What is the current outstanding balance on your homeloan? £

What is the current outstanding balance on your investment property loans?

Property 1	none	£
Property 2	none	£
Property 3	none	£
Property 4	none	£
Property 5	none	£
Property 6	none	£

What is the current outstanding balance on your other investment asset loans?

Investment 1	none	£
Investment 2	none	£
Investment 3	none	£
Investment 4	none	£
Investment 5	none	£
Investment 6	none	£

If you have any consumer debt, please enter details below.

Overdraft?	Insert description here	£
Car loans?	Insert description here	£
Credit Cards?	Insert description here	£
Store Cards?	Insert description here	£
Hire Purchase Debt?	Insert description here	£

If you have any other short-term debt, please list below.

Additional Debt 1	Insert description here	£
Additional Debt 2	Insert description here	£
Additional Debt 3	Insert description here	£
Additional Debt 4	Insert description here	£
Additional Debt 5	Insert description here	£
Additional Debt 6	Insert description here	£

Monthly outgoings

What is the monthly cost of your home loan?		£		per month
What is the monthly cost of your investment mortgages?				
Property 1	none	£		per month
Property 2	none	£		per month
Property 3	none	£		per month
Property 4	none	£		per month
Property 5	none	£		per month
Property 6	none	£		per month
What is the monthly cost of your other investment assets?				
Investment 1	none	£		per month
Investment 2	none	£		per month
Investment 3	none	£		per month
Investment 4	none	£		per month
Investment 5	none	£		per month
Investment 6	none	£		per month
What is the monthly cost of your pensions?				
Pension 1	none	£		per month
Pension 2	none	£		per month
Pension 3	none	£		per month
Pension 4	none	£		per month
What is the monthly cost of your savings?				
Savings 1	none	£		per month
Savings 2	none	£		per month
Savings 3	none	£		per month
Savings 4	none	£		per month
Savings 5	none	£		per month
Savings 6	none	£		per month
What is the monthly cost of your consumer debt?				
Overdraft?	none	£		per month
Car loans?	none	£		per month
Credit Cards?	none	£		per month
Store Cards?	none	£		per month
Hire Purchase Debt?	none	£		per month
What is the monthly cost of your other short-term debt?				
Additional Debt 1	none	£		per month
Additional Debt 2	none	£		per month
Additional Debt 3	none	£		per month
Additional Debt 4	none	£		per month
Additional Debt 5	none	£		per month
Additional Debt 6	none	£		per month

Financial freedom target

Income Details				
Insert your After-Tax Earned Income		£		
Insert your After-Tax Rental Income		£		
TOTAL NET INCOME		£	**0**	per annum
Non-Lifestyle Expenses				
Homeloan Mortgage	£ 0 monthly =	£	0	per annum
Investment Mortgages	£ 0 monthly =	£	0	per annum
Pension Contributions	£ 0 monthly =	£	0	per annum
Savings Plans	£ 0 monthly =	£	0	per annum
Consumer Debt	£ 0 monthly =	£	0	per annum
Other Short-term Debt	£ 0 monthly =	£	0	per annum
TOTAL NON-LIFESTYLE EXPENSES		£	**0**	per annum
Annual Lifestyle Income				
Total Net Income	less Total Non-Lifestyle Expenses	£	**0**	per annum

Financial Freedom Target

What age are you? [ ] In how any years do you plan to achieve your Financial Freedom? [ ] years

The future value of your Annual Lifestyle Income in years will be... £ **0** per annum

The Target Fund for your Financial Freedom is.... **£0**

Index